Higher Education in Mozambiq[ue]

A Case Study

Cover illustration
MALANGATANA MURAL FOR THE CENTRE FOR AFRICAN STUDIES
EDUARDO MONDLANE UNIVERSITY

Best known for his dramatic paintings, Malangatana (Valente Ngwenya) is one of Mozambique's most famous artists. He was one of the founders of the National Art Museum of Mozambique and is a strong supporter of the Nucleo de Arte, an associa- tion of painters, sculptors and other artists.

Malangatana has exhibited all over the world, both in collective and individual shows; his work is held in museums, galleries and individual collections in a large number of countries in Africa, Asia, Latin America, Europe and North America.

In 1999 Eduardo Mondlane University (UEM) asked him to paint a mural to com- memorate the thirtieth anniversary of the death of Eduardo Mondlane, the Mozambique liberation movement's founding President, who was assassinated by the Portuguese secret police.

The mural is in a quiet and green inner courtyard at the Centre for African Studies (CEA), already home to a small memorial to other outstanding African intellectuals who were victims of South African apartheid. Aquino de Braganca, director of the CEA, died in the unexplained plane crash that killed Samora Machel, the first President of independent Mozambique. Ruth First was blown up by a parcel bomb in her office at the CEA.

When Malangatana painted this mural, he was thinking about the spirits peopling the space and paying homage to them.

Higher Education in Africa

All titles published in association with Partnership for Higher Education in Africa

Daniel Mkude, Brian Cooksey & Lisbeth Levey
Higher Education in Tanzania
A Case Study

Nakanyike B. Musisi
& Nansozi K. Muwanga
Makerere University in Transition 1993–2000
Opportunities & Challenges

Mouzinho Mário, Peter Fry, Lisbeth Levey
& Arlindo Chilundo
Higher Education in Mozambique
A Case Study

Higher Education in Mozambique

A Case Study

Mouzinho Mário
Assistant Professor of Education
& Dean of Faculty of Education
Eduardo Mondlane University

Peter Fry
Professor of Anthropology
University of Rio de Janeiro

Lisbeth A. Levey
Director
Project for Information Access and Connectivity

Arlindo Chilundo
Director of Planning
Eduardo Mondlane University

Published in association with
Partnership for Higher Education in Africa

James Currey
OXFORD

Imprensa & Livraria Universitária
Universidade Eduardo Mondlane
MAPUTO

Partnership for Higher Education in Africa
New York University
The Steinhardt School of Education
Department of Administration, Leadership,
and Technology
239 Greene Street
New York, New York 10011, USA

Published by

James Currey Ltd
73 Botley Road
Oxford
OX2 0BS, UK

Imprensa & Livraria Universitária
Universidade Eduardo Mondlane
Campus Universitário
Edifício 3, CP 1840
Maputo, Mozambique

with the support of the Partnership for Higher Education in Africa,
an initiative of Carnegie Corporation of New York, The Ford Foundation, the John D.
and Catherine T. MacArthur Foundation, and the Rockefeller Foundation. The views
expressed are those of the authors and not necessarily the foundations that funded
this work.

1 2 3 4 5 07 06 05 04 03

British Library Cataloguing in Publication Data
Higher education in Mozambique : a case study. - (Higher
    education in Africa)
    1. Education, Higher - Mozambique 2. Education and state -
    Mozambique 3. Universities and colleges - Mozambique
    4. Educational change - Mozambique
    I. Mário, Mouzinho II. Fry, Peter III. Levey, Lisbeth A. IV. Chilundo, Arlindo
    IV. Partnership for Higher Education in Africa
    378.6'79

ISBN 0-85255-430-3 Paper

Library of Congress Cataloging-in-Publication Data is available

Typeset in 11/14 Monotype Photina
by Long House Publishing Services, Cumbria, UK
Printed and bound in Britain
by Woolnough, Irthlingborough

Contents

1   Introduction

2   Historical Background

3   Students: Access & Equity

4   Teaching Staff

5   Relevance, Quality, Quantity

List of Tables

List of Figures

List of Acronyms

AC	Academic Council
ACIPOL	Police Academy
ADEA	Association for the Development of Education in Africa
BUSCEP	Basic Science University Program
CDS/ISIS	Free bibliographic software package developed by UNESCO
CCRC	Central Commission for Curriculum Reform, Eduardo Mondlane University
CDDI	Centre for Documentation and Information, Catholic University of Mozambique
CD-ROM	Compact Disc-Read Only Memory
CHEPS	Centre for Higher Education Policy Studies, University of Twente
CIDOC	Centre for Information and Documentation
CIS	Centre for International Cooperation, Free University of Amsterdam
CIUEM	Informatics Centre, Eduardo Mondlane University
CNES	National Council for Higher Education
DGIS	Netherlands Directorate General for International Cooperation
DSD	Directorate for Documentation Services, Eduardo Mondlane University
DSS	Social Services Directorate, Eduardo Mondlane University
EDDI	Education and Democracy for Development Initiative, a USAID programme
EMUNet	Eduardo Mondlane University Network
ENM	Nautical School of Mozambique
ESES	Higher School of Education at Santarém
FRELIMO	Front for the Liberation of Mozambique
FUA	Free University of Amsterdam
HEI	Higher Education Institution
ICT	Information and Communications Technologies
IDRC	International Development Research Centre (Canada)
ISCTEM	Higher Institute of Sciences and Technology of Mozambique
ISP	Higher Pedagogical Institute, now Pedagogical University
ISPU	Higher Polytechnic and University Institute

ISRI	Higher Institute for International Relations
ISUTC	Higher Institute of Transport and Communications
IT	Information technology
LAN	Local Area Network
MT	Metacal, Mozambican currency (pl. metacais; MT 1,000=US$0.05)
MESCT	Ministry of Higher Education, Science and Technology
NORAD	Norwegian Agency for Development Cooperation
ODC	Organization for Distance Learning
PPI	Indicative Prospective Plan
RENAMO	Mozambican National Resistance
RUMA	Reform of University Management and Administration
SAREC	Swedish Agency for Research Cooperation
SDNP	Sustainable Development Networking Programme
SIDA	Swedish International Development Cooperation Agency
STADEP	Staff Development Project, Eduardo Mondlane University
UC	University Council
UCM	Catholic University of Mozambique
UEM	Eduardo Mondlane University
UMBB	Mussa bin Bik University
UNAM	University of Namibia
UNDP	United Nations Development Programme
UP	Pedagogical University
USAID	United States Agency for International Development
USIS	United States Information Service
VSAT	Very Small Aperture Terminal

Preface to the Series

The Partnership for Higher Education in Africa began as an affirmation of the ability of African universities to transform themselves and promote national development. We, the presidents of four US foundations – Carnegie Corporation of New York, The Ford Foundation, the John D. and Catherine T. MacArthur Foundation and the Rockefeller Foundation – came together out of a common belief in the future of African universities. Our interest in higher education proceeds from a simple faith that an independent scholarly community supported by strong universities goes hand-in-hand with a healthy, stable democracy. Universities are vitally important to Africa's development. Their crucial activities in research, intellectual leadership and developing successive generations of engaged citizens will nourish social, political and economic transformation in Africa. By pooling our resources, the foundations will help advance the reform of African universities and accelerate the development of their countries.

Much of sub-Saharan Africa has suffered deep stagnation over the last two decades and is staggering under the weight of domestic and international conflict, disease (especially the plague of HIV/AIDS), poverty, corruption and natural disasters. Its universities – once shining lights of intellectual excitement and promise – suffered from an enormous decline in government resources for education. In the last half of the last decade, however, things began to change in a number of countries. Our interest was captured by the renewal and resurgence that we saw in several African nations and at their universities, brought about by stability, democratization, decentralization and economic liberalization. Within these universities a new generation of leadership has stepped forward to articulate a vision for their institutions, inspiring confidence among those who care about African higher education. The case studies found that while the universities represented in these volumes have widely varying contexts and traditions, they are engaged in broad reform: examining and revising their planning processes, introducing new techniques of financial management, adopting new technologies, reshaping course structures and pedagogy and reforming practices of governance.

The first three case studies, on Makerere University and on the systems of higher education in Mozambique and Tanzania, focus on three of the six sub-Saharan countries that the Partnership has selected for concentration: Ghana, Mozambique, Nigeria, South Africa, Tanzania and Uganda. These six were chosen because their universities were initiating positive change, developing a workable planning process and demonstrating genuine commitment to national capacity building, in contexts of national reform.

The studies commissioned by the Partnership were carried out under the leadership of local scholars, using a methodology that incorporates feedback from the institutions under study and involving a broad range of stakeholders.

The publication of the first three case studies in this series is closely in line with the major aims of the Partnership:

- generating and sharing information about African universities and higher education
- supporting universities seeking to transform themselves
- enhancing research capacity on higher education in Africa
- promoting collaboration among African researchers, academics and university administrators

The studies are the product of the foundations' support for conceptual work that generates information about African higher education and university issues. Through the case studies, the foundations hope to promote a wider recognition of the importance of universities to African development. The publication of additional studies is planned, together with an essay on crosscutting themes from the case studies.

The foundations together have contributed US$62.3 million,

through December 2001, to fund higher education reform efforts in the targeted countries and institutions involved. The conceptual work supported by the individual foundations, working together in partnership towards a common vision, seeks to ensure the strengthening of institutional capacity for research on higher education in Africa and the wide dissemination of African research output.

We hope that the publication of these case studies will help advance the state of knowledge about higher education in Africa and support the movement for university reform on the continent. Equally significant, the process of our involvement in the case studies has enhanced our own understanding and helped the foundations focus future efforts of the Partnership. Interest in higher education in Africa has grown since the Partnership was launched in 2000. In this way, the Partnership not only uses its own resources but also acts as a catalyst to generate the support of others, on the continent and elsewhere, for African universities as vital instruments for development. We see these case studies as a critical step in the process of regeneration and transformation.

Vartan Gregorian, President
CARNEGIE CORPORATION OF NEW YORK

Susan Berresford, President
THE FORD FOUNDATION

Jonathan Fanton, President
JOHN D. AND CATHERINE T. MACARTHUR FOUNDATION

Gordon Conway, President
ROCKEFELLER FOUNDATION

Acknowledgements

Throughout this study we have been fortunate to count on the help and encouragement of a large number of people. They are listed with our gratitude in Appendix 1.

In particular, however, we would like to express our gratitude to the lecturers, administrators, librarians and students at all the institutions that received us and answered our many, often impertinent, questions with such frankness. In addition to institutions located in Maputo, we made visits to Beira, Quelimane, Nampula and, after a long and eventful train journey, Cuamba, where UCM has established a Faculty of Agriculture. We are more than grateful for the warm welcome we were given in these institutions and would like to thank them for their wholehearted cooperation. In addition, we thank the Ford Foundation and the Rockefeller Foundation for their financial and intellectual support.

Finally, we thank our efficient and dedicated research assistants, Bhangy Cassy, Lídia Titos Pedro, Osvaldo Camacho Andrade and Sandra Bernardo Guiamba.

1 Introduction

Of all the countries in southern Africa, Mozambique is probably the one that has experienced the most dramatic changes over the past 30 years. Gaining independence in 1975, it was one of the last Portuguese colonies. From 1975 to the mid-1980s, it embarked on an extremely ambitious socialist programme designed to bring about rapid and equitable development. But the Cold War and South Africa's determination to maintain apartheid and to destabilize the alternative society that Mozambique represented led to a bloody civil war, which ended only in 1992. Since then, Mozambique has marched forward into the 'new world order' and is now regarded as one of the most successful African attempts at structural adjustment.

During this period, higher education has undergone concomitantly dramatic changes. With the exodus of the Portuguese in 1975, Mozambique's only university lost most of its teaching staff and was obliged to play its part in developing skilled manpower for the socialist experiment. Nonetheless, during the period of the civil war and economic decline, the higher education sector expanded. Eduardo Mondlane University (UEM) was joined by two new governmental higher education institutions (HEIs) – the Higher Pedagogical Institute (ISP) and the Higher Institute for International Relations (ISRI). The end of the war and the socialist period heralded the inauguration of five non-governmental HEIs, the Higher Polytechnic and University Institute (ISPU), the Higher Institute of Sciences and Technology of Mozambique (ISCTEM), the Higher Institute of Transport and Communications (ISUTC), the Catholic University of Mozambique (UCM) and the Mussa bin Bik Islamic University (UMBB). Two new governmental institutions of higher education came into being during this period – the Nautical School of Mozambique (ENM) and the Police Academy (ACIPOL).

While the relative merits of private and public educational

1

institutions are vigorously debated, there is widespread consensus on the social significance of higher education in Mozambique. Despite the rapid growth of its economy in recent years, Mozambique continues to be one of the poorest countries in the world. Sustained economic growth is critically important for social development and the reduction of high levels of poverty. Yet Mozambique still suffers from a critical shortage of highly qualified professional skills that are fundamental for the development and execution of appropriate public policies, for effective leadership throughout society and for the training of successive generations of professionals and educators. It also suffers from acute regional disparities in wealth, development and qualified human resources, leading to all provincial governments and civic leaders demanding institutions of higher education in their regions. This combination of factors has led the government to attach great importance to higher education, inaugurating the Ministry of Higher Education, Science and Technology (MESCT). The new ministry is charged with devising an overall plan for higher education in Mozambique, deciding on the relative roles of governmental and non-governmental institutions and the most appropriate utilization of public funding.

The emergence of non-governmental universities has led to passionate debate on the nature of higher education in Mozambique. On the one side, there are those who are highly critical of non-governmental institutions of higher education. For them, the private institutions are suspect because they are motivated by market forces (and religious ones, in the case of the Catholic and Islamic universities) and are therefore little interested in the wider demands of university education in a secular society. They are also accused of weakening the governmental institutions by offering more attractive salaries to their faculty members who, as a consequence, dedicate less of their time to research or to their students at governmental institutions. On the other side, the proponents of a diverse field of higher education in Mozambique defend the emergence of non-governmental institutions, arguing that they bring healthy competition to the field, lead to a growth in the number of university places without cost to government and society and stimulate greater regional equity by bringing higher education to the provinces.

The field of higher education in Mozambique is in great flux and provides the scenario for considerable dispute. This study is therefore not a straightforward account of a stable system. Rather it tries to describe and analyse a rapidly changing field and the various positions within it. To do this we have used the following methodology.

(i) **Bibliography.** Eduardo Mondlane University and the Government of Mozambique have produced a wealth of statistical data over the years and have commissioned a number of reports on aspects of the higher education field (see References). We have utilized this information extensively, in particular the government's own *Strategic Plan of Higher Education in Mozambique, 2000–2010*. This excellent document provides a wealth of statistical information that facilitated our own work. The bibliography contains much more information on the governmental institutions (and of these, in particular, the UEM) than on the non-governmental institutions, which have emerged much more recently.

(ii) **Student survey.** While available statistical information on staff, students and financing is of relatively high quality, it became clear to us that there is little reliable information on the students' point of view. We therefore designed a questionnaire to be administered to students in governmental and non-governmental HEIs. The questionnaire was divided into three parts. The first part contained questions about students' demographic and socio-economic backgrounds. The second focused on students' satisfaction/dissatisfaction with the teaching and learning conditions in their institutions. The third asked students to provide suggestions for improving the functioning of libraries and other sources of information. The questionnaire combined closed and open-ended questions.

In all, 1,074 students enrolled in different HEIs responded to the questionnaire. This corresponds to nearly 10 per cent of the total higher education student population of Mozambique (nearly 11,000 students). A nonprobability sampling method allowed us to select a stratified sample of second-, third- and fifth-year students.[1] Although we did not select a random sample, we are satisfied that the characteristics of the students mirror the student population as a whole.

Of the total number of respondents, 384 (35.8 per cent) were female and 690 (64.2 per cent) male. The largest proportion of respondents came from UEM and UCM, with 53.5 and 21.7 per cent of respondents, respectively, followed by ISCTEM and ISPU (9.7 and 8.6 per cent of respondents, respectively). The percentage of male respondents from governmental HEIs was considerably higher than from non-governmental ones: 74, 70.2 and 65.2 per cent from UEM, UP and ISRI, respectively. In contrast, the percentage of female respondents from non-governmental HEIs was higher than governmental ones: 67.4, 61.5 and 36.9 per cent from ISPU, ISCTEM and UCM, respectively. For logistical reasons the sample does not include students from the UCM Faculty of Agriculture campus in Cuamba, Niassa, nor the ISPU campus in Quelimane, Zambezia.

(iii) **Interviews and observation.** The third technique adopted was designed to fill another lacuna in the bibliography. We felt that visits to all the HEIs in Mozambique would help us bring life to the statistics and reveal important information about the philosophy and values of those responsible for the various institutions. Since most of our own knowledge and experience had been gained in the governmental institutions, especially the UEM, we made a considerable effort to visit all the non-governmental institutions and the provincial branches of the governmental Pedagogical University. This included visits to Beira, Quelimane, Nampula and Cuamba, where UCM has established a Faculty of Agriculture.

The study is divided into eight chapters. The second chapter deals with the history of higher education in Mozambique and contains a brief description of the field of higher education as it stands now. The third looks at students, with special reference to questions of access and equity. This chapter makes extensive use of the student survey to assess their regional, socio-economic and cultural status in the various HEIs. The fourth chapter is centred on the teachers, their nationalities, qualifications and needs and their distribution among the various institutions. The fifth examines the teaching process – what is taught, where and how. It includes a discussion of relevance and quality and describes the measures taken to address high dropout rates and low rates of graduation. The student survey was utilized to understand how students perceive the teaching and learning environment in distinct institutions and particular disciplines. The sixth chapter consists of a description and analysis of information and communication technologies (ICT), including libraries, within the various institutions of higher learning. Chapter 7 examines the governance and financing of higher education institutions in Mozambique, with a preliminary comparison between non-governmental and governmental institutions. The final chapter sums up the findings of the study and makes tentative recommendations for action.

Note

1   E.E. Edwards et al. (1997: 62) contend that the minimum sample size needed from a population of 15,000 students at 95 per cent confidence and with 3 per cent margin of error is 997.

2 Historical Background[1]

The last years of colonialism – a university for colonialists & *assimilados*

In 1962, soon after the start of the African wars of independence, the Portuguese government founded the first institution of higher education in Mozambique. General University Studies of Mozambique, as it was called, began with courses in education, medicine, agronomy, forestry, veterinary sciences and civil, mining, electrical and chemical engineering. By 1968, when it became Lourenço Marques University, it had acquired departments of theoretical and applied mathematics, physics, chemistry, biology and geology. As the war for independence intensified, the university expanded to include courses in Roman philology, history, geography, economics and metallurgical engineering.

The university catered to the sons and daughters of Portuguese colonists. Although the Portuguese government preached non-racism and advocated the assimilation of its African subjects to the Portuguese way of life, the notorious deficiencies of the colonial education system established under Portuguese rule ensured that very few Africans would ever succeed in reaching university level. In spite of Portugal's attempts to counter international criticism of racism in its colonies by expanding African educational opportunity in the late 1960s and early 1970s, only about 40 black Mozambican students – less than 2 per cent of the student body – had entered the University of Lourenço Marques by independence in 1975. The state, industry, commerce and the university continued to depend heavily on the Portuguese and their descendants.

Independence & socialism – central planning requires a utilitarian university

With the Revolution of the Carnations in Portugal in April 1974, Portuguese universities, including Lourenço Marques

University, came to a standstill, as many lecturers and their students left to undertake political activities.

When the university reopened in January 1975, the staff and student body had been severely depleted, owing to the exodus of Portuguese colonists fearful of an African government with socialist tendencies. Student numbers fell from 2,433 in 1975 to 750 in 1978, while the Mozambican teaching staff was reduced to a mere ten. Indeed, soon after independence in June 1975, the Front for the Liberation of Mozambique (FRELIMO), which had been assisted by the Soviet bloc during the war for independence, adopted a Marxist-Leninist form of government, issuing in a period of central planning. The Indicative Prospective Plan (PPI), drawn up in 1980 after country-wide discussion, aimed to bring Mozambique into the modern world in the space of ten years. The educational system was nationalized, and the university was renamed in honour of Eduardo Mondlane, an anthropologist and first president of FRELIMO. The rector, Fernando Ganhão, a historian who had won his spurs in the war for independence, thwarted moves to close the university – it was regarded by some as an unnecessary expense – taking measures to adapt it to the daunting task of rapidly training cadres to implement the socialist programme.

To justify its existence, the university adopted a utilitarian stance, training human resources for what were considered to be the pressing needs of the new socialist economy. Courses considered of lesser priority and which had very few students were closed, such as biology, chemistry, physics, geology, mathematics, geography, history, modern languages and educational sciences. Some of the teachers in these disciplines were deployed to the pre-entry propaedeutic (preparatory) courses designed to augment the number of university entrants. To enable the government to expand the education system, the university also trained secondary teachers in the Faculty of Education established in 1980. The

Faculty of Marxism-Leninism came into being to provide instruction to all university students, and the Faculty for Combatants and Vanguard Workers was inaugurated to enable party cadres to acquire higher education. The university also acquired the Museum of Natural History, the Historical Archive and the Mozambican Institute for Scientific Research, which later became the Centre for African Studies. Scientists from the Soviet bloc and sympathizers (*cooperantes*) from all over the world filled the shortage of trained teaching staff. During those heady years, individual careers and vocations were subordinated to the national interest. The Ministry of Education assigned students to what were considered appropriate courses of study for them. On graduation they were similarly allocated to positions within government and party structures. While a number of Mozambicans studied abroad in western Europe, the majority during this period studied in universities in East Germany, the Soviet Union, Czechoslovakia and Bulgaria.

Mozambique's independence, its socialist orientation and its support for South African and Zimbabwean liberation movements provoked the wrath of Rhodesia and South Africa which, one after the other, provided financial and logistical support to the rebel Mozambican National Resistance (RENAMO). Continuous violent war compounded by drought and the growing unpopularity of FRELIMO's socialist programme brought the Mozambican economy to its knees. By the mid-1980s, Mozambique had become the poorest country in the world, with an estimated annual income per capita of US$60. As the war progressed and government revenues declined, morale foundered and the university lost all possibility of research outside the city of Maputo, while buildings, laboratories and other facilities became increasingly decrepit.

In spite of these economic setbacks, the higher education sector expanded with the establishment of two further public institutions of higher learning: the Higher Pedagogical Institute

(ISP) in 1985 and the Higher Institute for International Relations (ISRI) in 1986. The former, which was charged with the training of secondary schoolteachers, took over the role of the UEM's Faculty of Education which was duly closed. Occupying the buildings of what had been a technical college during the colonial period, the ISP catered to schoolteachers who had been denied access to higher education during the first years of independence. Since the demand for trained personnel far outstripped the number of university graduates, a large number of ISP graduates preferred gainful employment in the private sector to returning to badly paid and low-status school teaching jobs. ISRI, which had been conceived by President Joaquim Chissano while he was foreign minister, was born under the aegis of the Ministry of Foreign Affairs and made responsible for training future diplomats.

Peace, democracy, a market economy & the emergence of non-governmental institutions of higher education

As the government sued for peace and as the Soviet bloc crumbled, Mozambique's relations of dependence on the wider world shifted from the former Soviet Union and East Germany to Europe and the United States. The government began to relax its socialist programme, accepting loans from the International Monetary Fund and the World Bank from 1987 onwards. It also began to shift from socialism to democracy, and a new liberal constitution was adopted in 1990. After years of negotiations under the aegis of the Catholic Church in Rome, FRELIMO and RENAMO signed a peace accord in October 1992. In 1995 the first democratic general elections were held.

In February 1990, Dr Narciso Matos, a chemist who had studied as an undergraduate at Lourenço Marques University and who had completed his doctorate in the former East Germany, became the first black rector of Eduardo Mondlane University. Soon after taking up his post, the new rector was confronted by a student strike. At a meeting of the entire university chaired by the rector in the university gymnasium, President Chissano listened to a hard-hitting speech by the student leader, who contrasted the ostentatious wealth and well-being of the country's leaders with the poverty of the students and the people as a whole.

Although this strike does not figure in the official history of the university, the students to whom we spoke consider it crucial in marking the changes under way in the country and in drawing the attention of government to the problems of higher education. Theirs was the second strike since independence (the first occurred in 1989), marking the beginning of the emergence of an active civil society. The government did in fact take the strike seriously and adopted measures to increase support to the university. But more importantly, the frank confrontation between the students and the authorities signalled the emergence of the freedom of expression that had been seriously curtailed throughout the colonial period and the post-independence war. It is significant that this signal came from the Eduardo Mondlane University. It is also significant that shortly afterwards the university took important steps to diagnose its ills and to prepare a strategic plan for their resolution, even though there was no direct relationship between the strikes and the planning process.

By the mid-1990s times had changed again. Multi-party democracy had become a reality, and instead of a war-torn country in need of compassion and aid, Mozambique presented an image to the world of an attractive opportunity for investment. The macroeconomic situation became increasingly buoyant, with annual GDP growth moving into double figures and the privatization of state-owned firms advancing apace. Concomitantly, the provision of medical and educational

11

services ceased to be a monopoly of the state. Private clinics and secondary schools emerged in the early 1990s, followed by private schools and institutions of higher learning.

Anticipating these changes, the government introduced legislation governing higher education in the early 1990s. In 1991 a government 'diploma' instituted competitive examinations for access to higher education, bringing to an end the subjugation of personal careers to state decision-making. In 1993, Parliament approved the creation of the National Council for Higher Education. Composed of rectors of all institutions of higher education and chaired by the Minister of Education, the Council was charged with evaluating applications for the establishment of HEIs and advising the Council of Ministers, which remained ultimately responsible for approving the establishment of new institutions and for all policy decisions.

Although at this time there had been talk of rationalizing the higher education sector by promoting cooperation between the three government-owned Maputo-based institutions,[2] the opposite course was adopted. In 1995 the ISP was given full university status, becoming the Pedagogical University (UP), and the Higher Institute for International Relations also acquired university status when its rector was given a seat on the National Council for Higher Education.

The first non-governmental institutions of higher education, ISPU and UCM, emerged in August 1996. They were followed in 1997 by ISCTEM and in 2000 by ISUTC and the Islamic UMBB.

The expansion of the sector also involved steps to decentralize. In 1990, the ISP set up a branch in the second city of Beira, with a course in mathematics. Five years later, UP established another branch in the city of Nampula.

The Catholic University was radical in its desire to decentralize. In fact, decentralization was its raison d'être. In 1992, as peace negotiations between FRELIMO and RENAMO seemed doomed to failure, Dom Jaime Gonçalves, the Archbishop of Beira, promised that if peace was restored the Catholic Church would establish a university in Beira in order to provide higher education for the people of the centre and north of the country. Dom Jaime understood that an important component of the conflict between FRELIMO and RENAMO was the ancient antagonism between the south and the centre and north of the country. True to Dom Jaime's promise, the Catholic University established its headquarters in Beira. Faculties of education and law were located in the capital of Nampula province, while the faculty of agriculture was installed in the small Niassa town of Cuamba, which is linked to Nampula by a daily passenger railway service. The Maputo-based ISPU established a branch in Quelimane, the capital of the province of Zambezia and home town of its rector, Dr Lourenço do Rosário. There, it offers courses in law and business administration.

Currently the field of higher education in Mozambique consists of nine functioning HEIs, plus the Nautical School of Mozambique, which is more or less dormant.

In most government publications HEIs are classified as public and private. Since all of them are public in the sense that the government approves them to provide public education, this classification is not entirely appropriate. It is important, however, to distinguish between forms of ownership. Five HEIs are state-owned and controlled; we shall refer to these as governmental institutions. Two are owned by religious denominations; we shall refer to them as 'denominational institutions'. Private individuals and corporations own the remaining three; we shall refer to them as 'for-profit institutions'. We will refer to both the denominational and the for-profit institutions as non-governmental higher education institutions. The most general characteristics of these institutions are summarized in Table 1.

Table 1: Summary of HEIs in Mozambique, 1999

Name	Year founded	Location and branches	Number of courses	Student numbers
Governmental institutions				
Eduardo Mondlane University (UEM)	1962	Maputo	22	6,800
Pedagogical University (UP)	1985	Maputo	12	1,987 (total)
		Beira	5	
		Nampula	12	3
Higher Institute for International Relations (ISRI)	1986	Maputo	1	234
Nautical School of Mozambique (ENM)	1991	Maputo	3	0
Police Academy (ACIPOL)	1999	Maputo	2	128
Denominational institutions				
Catholic University of Mozambique (UCM)	1996	Beira	3	1,035 (total)
		Nampula	2	
		Cuamba	1	
Mussa bin Bik University (UMBB)	1998	Nampula	No info.	No info.
For-profit institutions				
Higher Polytechnic and University Institute (ISPU)	1995	Maputo	8	919
		Quelimane	2	
Higher Institute of Sciences and Technology of Mozambique (ISCTEM)	1996 1996	Maputo Maputo	7 7	644 644
Institute of Transport and Communications (ISUTC)	1999	Maputo	3 ?	

14

This table may suggest a stability that is illusory. The field of higher education is in a state of great flux. To date it has developed on an *ad hoc* basis without overarching guidelines. Most writing in the field of higher education distinguishes between private and public institutions, which we have chosen to call governmental and non-governmental. This is an important distinction. The most obvious difference between these two categories is the way they are financed. The non-governmental institutions receive no direct support from the state and depend largely on students' fees. While these are almost purely nominal in the governmental institutions (about US$34 per term if the students take six disciplines), they vary between US$150 and US$250 per month in the non-governmental ones. There are other differences which cut across the governmental/non-governmental divide. It might be argued, for example, that there are only two universities in the strict sense of the term, one of them governmental (UEM), the other denominational (UCM). The government's Pedagogical University is in fact more like a teachers' training college. All the other institutions are really clusters of faculties (the non-governmental ISPU, ISCTEM and ISUTC), or, in the case of the governmental ISRI, a single faculty.

We shall examine the particularities of these institutions in regard to the broad questions of access and equity, the generation and transmission of knowledge, the relevance and quality of courses taught and the way in which they are governed.

What has changed the field of higher education most dramatically is the end of the state monopoly over the production and transmission of knowledge at all levels of society. For many (the authors of this study included), the vitality of the non-governmental fee-paying institutions of higher education was beyond imagination as little as ten years or so ago. For many of these, especially those educated during the socialist years, the non-governmental institutions (with the possible exception of the Catholic University) are seen as undesirable excrescences that sap the lifeblood of the public institutions and are governed more by Mammon than Socrates. For others, they are a welcome addition to the field of higher education, providing alternatives to the older institutions and bringing a spirit of healthy competition to an arena that has been complacent for too long. It is hoped that the pages that follow will contribute to this debate. Whatever conclusion the reader may reach, there is little doubt about the vitality, creativity and social importance of higher education in contemporary Mozambique.

Notes   1   This chapter draws substantially on Fry and Utu (1999).
2   In 1995 a World Bank-funded research team which included representatives of UEM, UP and ISRI strongly recommended resource sharing
among the three Maputo-based HEIs, going so far as to suggest unifying
them into a federal system (Holsinger et al., 1994).

3 Students: Access & Equity

Supply & demand

All forms of education are a scarce resource in Mozambique, with a drastic funnelling at each successive higher stage in the educational system. The 1998 United Nations Development Programme (UNDP) *Human Development Report* estimated the adult literacy rate in Mozambique at 40.1 per cent, with the rate among females (23.3 per cent) less than half the male rate of 57.7 per cent. According to the 1997 census the overall gross enrolment rate was 66.8 per cent in primary education, falling to 0.3 per cent in higher education, with the female rates being considerably lower than male rates (Table 2).

Table 2: Gross enrolment rates in Mozambique, 1997 (%)

	Total	Men	Women
Primary education	66.8	75.7	57.7
Secondary education	6.9	8.2	5.6
Technical education	0.8	1.1	0.5
Higher education	0.3	0.5	0.2

Source: *Strategic Plan of Higher Education* (2000).

The authors of the *Strategic Plan of Higher Education* estimate a total school population of over 2 million in 1998, with 96 per cent of enrolment at the primary level (Table 3).

All those who have completed 12 years of formal education may apply for university entrance. They include those who graduate from the pre-university secondary schools, both governmental and non-governmental, and those who have attended technical institutes. The non-governmental HEIs have instituted pre-university courses ('zero semester' at the for-profits and the propaedeutic year at the UCM), which are open to all applicants. The public universities, however, only admit students who have passed their entrance examinations. The preparatory year at UCM is an integral part of the

17

Table 3: Public school population of Mozambique, 1998

| | Primary | | Secondary | | | Technical | | |
	1st level (Grades 1–5)	2nd level (Grades 6–7)	1st cycle (Grades 8–10)	2nd cycle (Grades 11–12)	Elemen-tary	Basic	Medium	Higher
Total	1,876,154	168,777	53,693	7,352	398	14,170	2,619	8,537
M	1,088,105	100,547	32,077	4,498	349	9,979	2,085	6,208
F	788,049	68,230	21,616	2,854	49	4,191	534	2,329

Source: *Strategic Plan of Higher Education* (2000).

curriculum, whereas the zero semester at the for-profit institutions is not.

During the 1990s, university student numbers increased from fewer than 4,000 in 1990 to almost 12,000 in 1999 (Figure 1), and enrolment in governmental institutions more than doubled, from 3,750 in 1990 to 9,201 in 1999. The rapid increase from 1996 onwards is due to the opening of non-governmental institutions whose intake increased from 262 students in 1996 to 2,598 in 1999.

In spite of this growth, the demand for higher education is greater than the supply. The pre-university schools produce few graduates, but the number of candidates for university places is increased by those with diplomas from medium-level technical and vocational schools or teacher-training colleges. In 1999 there were 10,974 applicants for these 2,342 places. Very few potential candidates were denied access to higher education during the socialist years because the number of high-school graduates was very small. Until 1990 there were no university entrance examinations; everyone with a high-school or equivalent diploma was guaranteed access to UEM.

The candidate/vacancy ratio varies between governmental

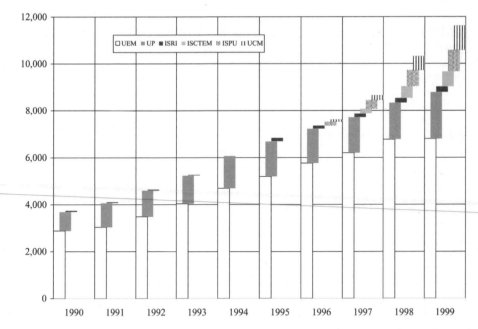

Figure 1: Number of students enrolled in HEIs, 1990–99

Source: *Strategic Plan of Higher Education* (2000).

and non-governmental HEIs and between specific university courses. At the governmental HEIs demand exceeds supply by ratios of 8:7 at UEM, 9:1 at ISRI, 9:4 at UP and 3:1 at ACIPOL. Admission rates in 1999 were 12.7, 11.0, 24.6 and 32.1 per cent, respectively. In contrast, UCM filled all its vacancies and rejected no candidates, while at ISCTEM there were 13 per cent fewer candidates than places. Certain university departments are more sought after than others. Table 4 shows that, at UEM, law, economics and management and computer science attract more than five candidates for each place, while geology, chemistry, chemical engineering, physics and meteorology attract less than one candidate per place.

In spite of the growth in the number of university places, students in HEIs represent a microscopic segment in relation

19

Table 4: Places offered, candidates & candidate place/ratio, UEM, 2000

Course	Places	Candidates	Candidate per place ratio
Law	100	1062	10.6
Economics and Management	75	486	6.5
Computer Science	37	228	6.2
Architecture	24	120	5.0
Civil Engineering	40	189	4.7
Electrical Engineering	50	222	4.4
Medicine	90	277	3.1
Veterinary Science	25	64	2.6
Biology	5	65	2.6
Agronomy and Forestry	100	230	2.3
History	35	69	2.0
Linguistics	35	67	1.9
Geography	35	60	1.7
Social Sciences	75	967	1.0
Mechanical Engineering	50	48	1.0
Geology	30	27	0.9
Chemistry	30	24	0.8
Chemical Engineering	35	21	0.6
Physics and Meteorology	30	6	0.2

Source: *UEM Report on Entrance Examinations* (1999).

to the population as a whole. Only 0.16 per cent of the age cohort 20–25, or 40 in every 100,000 inhabitants, study at HEIs. Table 5 shows how this proportion compares with other countries in the region and the world. In Zimbabwe and Botswana, for example, there are 638 and 596 university students for every 100,000 inhabitants.

Within this diminutive proportion of Mozambicans who enter HEIs, certain categories are less represented than others, in particular women, people from the centre and north of the country and the rural poor.

20

Table 5: Number of higher-education students per 100,000 inhabitants

Country	1985	1990	1996
United States	5,064	5,395	5,339
Netherlands	2,794	3,203	3,176
Brazil	1,158	1,081	1,094
Zimbabwe	368	496	638
Botswana	181	299	596
Mozambique	11	37	40

Source: UNESCO *Statistical Yearbook* (1993, 1996 and 1998)

Distribution of the sexes

Women are in a minority throughout the educational system (as seen in Table 2). Overall, however, the proportion of women has increased over recent years, from 2.6 men to one woman in 1997 to 1.8 men to one woman in 1999.

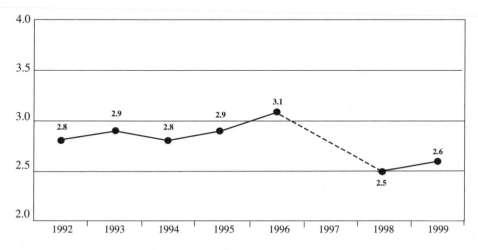

Figure 2: M/F ratio at all HEIs, 1992–9

Source: *Strategic Plan of Higher Education* (2000).

As Figure 2 shows, the proportion of female students gradually increased from 1992, the first year for which a gender breakdown is available. In general, the ratio of male to female students remained high (between 2.8 and 3.1 to 1) between 1990 and 1996, but fell to 2.5 and 2.6 to 1 in 1998 and 1999. This was partly due to the opening of private HEIs, where the proportion of female students is higher than at the public HEIs (43 per cent on average in private HEIs in 1999, compared with only 25 per cent in the public sector). Why the non-governmental HEIs should attract/accept a higher proportion of women is as yet a mystery. The *Strategic Plan of Higher Education* suggests that this may be the result of new social science courses opening at UEM and to the general amelioration of the social situation of women in Mozambique. Unlike the governmental institutions, and with the exception of a project promoting women students at ISPU's Quelimane branch, the non-profit HEIs have not taken a proactive stance on the disparities between male and female students. Teachers at the Catholic University, however, suggest that by moving out of Maputo they have attracted women students from families who would have hesitated to allow their daughters to travel to Maputo. In 2001, the majority of the students enrolled in the propaedeutic year of the new Faculty of Medicine in Beira were female.

Geography

Historically, the southern provinces (Maputo, Gaza and Inhambane) have been more developed than the central (Manica, Sofala, Tete and Zambezia) and northern provinces (Nampula, Niassa and Cape Delgado). They are closer to the capital, Maputo, and to the economic powerhouse of South Africa. They have a higher number of industrial and agricultural development projects; they are better served by roads and railways; and they boast a denser network of governmental and non-governmental primary and secondary schools and HEIs. Needless to say, the proportion of university students from the northern and central provinces is much lower than those from the south. According to the *Strategic Plan of Higher Education*, 60 per cent of university students come from the three southern provinces, 25 per cent from the central provinces and 15 per cent from the remaining three northern provinces. These proportions are in fact more seriously out of balance than they seem at first sight, when one takes into account that the populations of the north, centre and south represent 32.9 per cent, 41.2 per cent and 25.9 per cent of the total population of Mozambique, respectively.

Table 6: Percentage of university students by region, 1999

Area	% of total number of university students	% of total population
North	15	32.9
Centre	25	41.2
South	60	25.9

Source: *Strategic Plan of Higher Education* (2000).

Just as the coming of the non-governmental HEIs brought about an improvement in the ratio between the sexes, they have also reduced the geographical disparities, albeit mini-mally. Figure 3 shows that the proportion of students from the north and centre is slightly higher in the non-governmental institutions.

The fact that the non-governmental institutions have helped to reduce regional disparities can be attributed to the deliberate policy of the Catholic University to establish itself in the centre and the north and to ISPU's inauguration of a branch in the Zambezi capital of Quelimane.

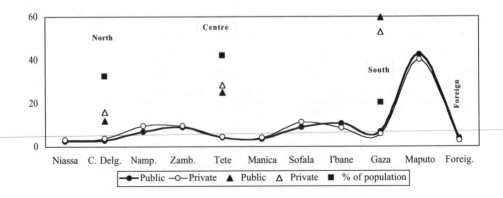

Figure 3: Region of origin of students entering HEIs, 1990–99

Source: *Strategic Plan of Higher Education* (2000).

Our visits to UCM's Faculty of Agriculture at Cuamba and the ISPU branch in Quelimane verified that these institutions do in fact cater mainly to students from the centre and the north, as shown in Figures 4 and 5. The establishment of HEIs in the centre and the north has economic, cultural and political significance. HEIs create jobs, raise local pride, encourage and promote debate on topics of national and regional importance, and establish libraries and information systems that the general public may utilize. It is difficult to underestimate the political importance of these institutions.

However, the problem of regional disparities is worsened by the tendency for students from the centre and the north studying in Maputo not to return to their home provinces after graduation. Measures to encourage student return may include, among others, increased job and professional develop-ment opportunities, social recognition, and access to credit and housing schemes for young graduates.

At the national seminar held in Maputo in July 2000 to discuss the Strategic Plan of Higher Education, every provin-cial delegate pleaded for the establishment of an HEI in his

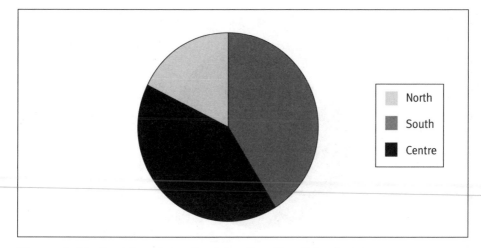

Figure 4: Students' region of origin, Faculty of Agriculture, Cuamba

Source: Student records.

(there were no women delegates) provincial capital. The discrepancies between the south, on the one hand, and the centre and north on the other, which were manifest during the civil war and which remain in the opposition between FRELIMO and RENAMO, continue to mobilize a high level of public opinion.

There is no official information on the social class of university students. However, our survey data lead us to believe that this is the most significant factor determining access to higher education in Mozambique. We took the educational level of fathers and mothers as the principal indicator of socio-economic position. Table 7 compares the educational level of parents of students at governmental and non-governmental HEIs.

As data from Table 7 show, almost 70 per cent of students' fathers have secondary education or more, as opposed to a mere 2.8 per cent of men in the population as a whole.

25

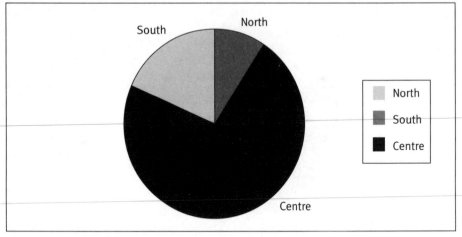

Figure 5: Students' region of origin, ISPU, Quelimane

Source: Student records.

Students' mothers show a similar pattern; about 50 per cent of students' mothers have secondary education or higher, as opposed to 0.9 per cent of women in the population as a whole. At the other end of the educational scale, we can see that while 89.3 per cent of Mozambican women and 78.8 per cent of Mozambican men have had no formal education, the percentages for the fathers and mothers of our surveyed students are about 8 and 2 per cent respectively.

It is interesting to note that the educational level of the parents of students at governmental institutions is slightly lower than that of the parents of students at non-governmental HEIs. In particular, 56.1 per cent of mothers of students at non-governmental HEIs have a secondary education and higher, as compared with only 49.1 per cent of the mothers of students at non-governmental HEIs.

Perhaps the most significant finding of our survey, however, relates to the linguistic preferences of students. In Mozambique as a whole, 38.9 per cent of the population is able to speak

Table 7: Mothers' & fathers' educational levels

Educational level	Governmental HEIs				Non-governmental HEIs				Mozambique	
	Mothers		Fathers		Mothers		Fathers		Women	Men
	Frequency	%	Frequency	%	Frequency	%	Frequency	%	%	
No education	46	8.2	16	2.8	32	9.4	5	1.4	8.3	78.8
Primary	240	42.7	162	28.5	118	34.6	113	32.5	9.8	18.5
Secondary	182	32.4	201	35.3	126	37.0	124	35.6	0.7	2
Technical	34	6.0	81	14.2	17	5.0	28	8.0	0.13	0.6
Higher	60	10.7	109	19.2	48	14.1	78	22.4	0.05	0.15
Total	562	100.0	569	100.0	341	100.0	348	10.0	100.0	100.0

Sources: Student survey; National Census (1997).

Portuguese, according to the 1997 census. Only 8.7 per cent utilizes the Portuguese language in their home environment. Among our sample of university students, however, 696 (64.8 per cent) claimed that Portuguese was their mother/parental tongue, while 673 (62.7 per cent) indicated that they always use Portuguese to communicate with their parents and other relatives, 228 (21.2 per cent) that they use Portuguese very often, and only 113 (10.5 per cent) that they use Portuguese only occasionally. A small minority of 23 (2.1 per cent) indicated that they never use Portuguese with their parents and other close relatives. Breaking down this linguistic data by HEI leads us to even more interesting speculation.

The proportion of students with Portuguese as their mother tongue is higher at the non-governmental HEIs than at the governmental ones. At ISPU, for example, as many as 83 per cent of the students claimed Portuguese as their mother tongue. This tends to confirm what the data on parents' educational levels suggest, namely, that students at non-governmental institutions come from segments of higher socio-economic status than students at governmental institutions. There are also marked differences among the governmental

Table 8: Mother language by HEI

| | Governmental HEIs | | | | | | Non-governmental HEIs | | | | | | | |
| | UEM | | UP | | ISRI | | UC | | ISCTEM | | ISPU | | Total | |
	Freq.	%	Freq.	%	Freq.	%	Freq.	%	Freq.	%	Freq.	%	Freq.	%
African	190	34	27	60	7	32	75	35	20	20	15	17	334	28
Portuguese	373	66	18	40	15	68	138	65	78	80	74	83	840	72
Total	563	100	45	100	22	100	213	100	98	100	89	100	1,174	100

Source: Student survey.

institutions. The proportion of African/Portuguese mother tongue at UEM and ISRI is very similar, at about 3.5 : 6.5. At UP, however, the ratio is inverted to 6 : 4. This suggests that the socio-economic status of UP students is lower than at other institutions and reinforces our suspicion that the majority of UP students are those who have failed to pass the entrance examination to UEM, while lacking the resources to enter non-governmental HEIs. On the other hand, UP may be used by dissatisfied teachers in primary and secondary schools as a pathway to escape the teaching profession. Looking at figures on the rural or urban origin of students in Table 9, the

Table 9: Origin of students by HEI (%)

| | Governmental | | | Non-governmental | | | |
| | | | | | Denomi-national | For-profit | |
	UEM	UP	ISRI	UCM	ISCTEM	ISPU	Average
No info.	2.8	2.1	4.3	10.3	4.8	6.5	4.9
Urban	57.2	27.7	52.2	51.1	66.3	73.9	56.8
Semi-rural	14.1	14.9	17.4	15.9	14.4	6.5	14
Rural	25.9	55.3	26.1	22.7	14.5	13.1	24.3

Source: Student survey.

28

hierarchy revealed by the language data is corroborated, and the special niche of the UP as home to poorer and more rural students is confirmed.

With regard to place of origin, the ratios at UEM and UP are inverted again. At UEM, for each student of urban origin there are 0.7 rural or semi-rural students. At UP we find 2.5 rural or semi-rural students for each student of urban origin. Amongst the non-governmental institutions, the Catholic University is marginally more rural, while ISPU and ISCTEM have the highest proportion of non-rural students (74 and 66 per cent respectively).

These data should not blind us to the fact that while there is a hierarchization of HEIs by social class, this is more dramatically the case in particular disciplines.

Table 10 shows the educational level of students' mothers by course, suggesting that law and medicine are the most prestigious and education the least.[1] The pattern is familiar: the courses of higher prestige that, in theory at least, equip

Table 10: Mothers' educational level by course of study (%)

	Below secondary level	Secondary level and above	No data
Agronomy	47.2	45.9	6.9
Arts	37.2	39.5	23.3
Economics and management	38.1	42.5	19.4
Education	61.6	41.6	39.1
Engineering	41.6	44.1	14.3
International relations	39.1	34	29.5
Law	34	49	17
Medicine	29.5	60.7	9.8
Natural sciences	58.5	31.7	9.8
Social sciences	42.5	42.5	15
Vet. medicine	60.9	30.4	8.7

Source: Student survey.

29

their graduates with greater chances of acquiring prestige and wealth tend to admit students from the more privileged segments of society.

Perhaps this has always been the case. During the socialist period, however, bright students from the less privileged sectors of society could win places in government secondary schools and then be sent to university by a watchful state. With the advent of the market economy and the inauguration of private schools and universities, this pattern has changed. Those parents who can afford to send their children to private secondary and pre-university schools can provide them with a greater chance of passing the increasingly competitive entrance examinations.

Table 11: Success rates of candidates for UEM, by private & public schools

	Private schools			Public schools		
	No. candidates	No. passed	% pass rate	No. candidates	No. passed	% pass rate
First exam	712	154	18.1	5,482	1,137	11.2

Source: UEM Report on Admissions Exams (1999c).

Data on the results of entrance examinations for 1999 confirm this hypothesis. The UEM entrance exam takes place in two phases. During the first phase successful candidates must achieve a certain minimum percentage in their exams. The second phase fills up available places, reducing the percentage necessary for admission. Table 11 shows that over 18 per cent of candidates from private schools passed the first phase of the entrance exam as opposed to about 11 per cent from public schools.

The evidence suggests that there is a growing tendency for the educational system as a whole, and the field of higher education in particular, to reproduce existing social in-equalities, particularly socio-economic ones. If measures are not taken to improve the chances of less privileged children (either by providing scholarships to private schools and/or in the long term strengthening the quality of governmental schools), we shall witness the consolidation of a closed socio-economic elite in Mozambique, concentrated geographically in Maputo.

Policies for improving access & equity

There are no systematic data on policies adopted to address the inequalities to which we have referred. One of our recommendations is that an evaluation of these policies be undertaken in order to learn lessons appropriate for the future.

There are initiatives, however, to address some aspects of socio-economic inequality. The principal tool for increasing the number of female students at UEM has been the award of scholarships. For the academic year 2000/01, a total of 198 scholarships were given to women students, with funding mainly from Scandinavian governments and the Mozambican government.

There are currently eight student residences at UEM. Of the 1,020 students living there, 909 (89 per cent) are scholarship holders, of whom only 106 (11.6 per cent) are female. The residential capacity of UEM has increased considerably during the last few years, from 733 to 1,051 beds (a 30 per cent increase). This was made possible by the construction of a new residential complex known as Colmeia (Phase I), the acquisition and rehabilitation of a new apartment building donated by the government and the rehabilitation of older residences. Funding for construction and rehabilitation came from the 'Capacity Building Project' that emanated from the UEM 1991 strategic plan *The Present and Perspectives for the Future*.

In this first UEM strategic plan, concern was expressed at

the fact that 61 per cent of students were from the more developed southern provinces of the country. To counter this imbalance, it was proposed to explore 'different alternatives such as setting aside a pool of openings in all the courses of study for students outside Maputo, together with an expansion of university housing and scholarships for such students' (UEM, 1991, Vol. 2: 36). As a result, of the 848 students living in eight student residences in January 2001, only 10 per cent came from Maputo, 18.2 per cent from Gaza and Inhambane, 56 per cent from Sofala, Manica, Tete and Zambezia, and 15.4 per cent from Nampula, Niassa and Cape Delgado.

Evidently the decision of the Catholic University to concentrate on the centre and north of the country was a deliberate, largely efficacious, decision to confront the historical imbalance. By the same token, the initiative of UP to establish branches in Nampula and Beira has had some effect on the geographic imbalance in higher education. The establishment of an ISPU branch in Quelimane was also a deliberate attempt to help develop the province of Quelimane. ISPU received five scholarships, two for university students and three for technical college students, from the Community Development Foundation that is presided over by Graça Machel.

The most interesting project we came across was in the province of Nampula. This Netherlands government-funded project in Nampula (called Nisomé, meaning 'let us study' in the local language, Emakua) is designed to provide scholarships to sons and daughters of residents of the province of Nampula. Composed of representatives of Nampula society including schoolmasters, religious leaders and local community leaders, the commission charged with examining applications has won a reputation for fairness. Candidates fill in a form, undergo interviews and then receive a visit from the commission to verify their economic data *in situ*. Scholarships are awarded on a kind of means test. The poorest students receive a full scholarship to cover fees, plus board and lodging. Less impoverished candidates receive a contribution commensurate with their needs.

Those who win scholarships from Nisomé agree to spend the same amount of time in Nampula after graduation that they took to obtain their degrees. Should they wish to break the contract, the scholarship is transformed into a low-interest loan.

The local provision of scholarships confronts all the problems that candidates from the centre and north of the country have habitually had to deal with. Because of poor communications and labyrinthine bureaucracy, many students from the north or centre who gain scholarships to UEM find out too late that they have won them. By that time they have been taken up by better informed candidates. Nisomé guarantees the easy flow of communication between candidates and HEIs and the kind of care that national schemes are unable to provide. Another advantage is that such a regional scholarship fund is able to accommodate students at all institutions of higher learning. Nisomé sends students to UEM, UP, UCM, ISPU and ISCTEM.

Distance learning

Distance learning is also regarded as an important means of expanding access to higher education in the country. According to the government strategic plan, distance learning will be introduced gradually. The first phase will comprise three priority actions:

* training personnel for the management of the system;
* developing resource centres to provide academic, logistical and technical support;
* creating pilot projects to ensure the development and sustainability of distance learning.

33

The first phase will culminate in the creation of an Organization for Distance Learning (ODL) and will be followed by either one or two of the following activities, depending on the model chosen:[2]

- development of courses and programmes by the institutions offering the resources, with the ODL responsible for the coordination of distance learning activities, training of personnel, research and quality assurance of the courses offered (model c);
- development of an open university with total responsibility for all distance learning systems resting with ODL (model d).

Notes

1   We have excluded disciplines with a very small number of students because they are not statistically significant.

2   Various models are under consideration, as follows.

a. Distance learning to be introduced in existing government or non-government HEIs with each institution developing its own human resources and infrastructure (the current trend).

b. Introduction of distance learning by a consortium of HEIs that would build the needed infrastructure, train the specialized human resources and set up a management steering committee. Each institution would be responsible for curriculum planning and design, production of teaching materials and evaluation of students' performance. Supervision would be either by a network of tutors managed by each institution or by the consortium. The consortium would be open to any institution offering distance learning at higher, medium or secondary education levels.

c. Distance learning to be coordinated by an autonomous institution established for that purpose with the responsibility of developing and managing appropriate infrastructures and offering training and methodologies at the institutions involved. This institution would be responsible for ensuring student supervision, whilst the other institutions would be responsible for the evaluation of students, keeping academic records and awarding certificates. The autonomous institution would also conduct research about distance learning, assess the production process and manage and monitor the courses and programmes offered. It would be the centre of excellence in distance learning systems and processes and would assist other institutions in the planning, design and evaluation of courses and programmes, and in the dissemination of the results of research undertaken and of the best national and foreign experiences in distance learning.

d. Introduction of distance learning to be undertaken by an autonomous institution to be created. Its nucleus would consist of lecturers from existing HEIs. The institution would be responsible for the management of infrastructure, planning, curriculum design and development, production of teaching materials, academic registration, supervision, evaluation and certification of students. This nucleus could evolve to become an open university.

4 Teaching Staff

Prior to the advent of non-governmental HEIs

As noted earlier, the gravest problem of Mozambican higher education at independence was the dramatic shortage of qualified teachers, owing to two factors: the exodus of the Portuguese and the lack of Portuguese investment in education for native Mozambicans.

To confront this situation, the university authorities adopted both short- and long-term perspectives. To resolve the short-term shortage of qualified instructors, faculty members were recruited from countries all over the world that were sympathetic to Mozambican independence. Senior faculty members recall the polyglot nature of the Eduardo Mondlane University during the first years of independence; it was truly a Tower of Babel. The long-term strategy involved recruiting promising young Mozambicans with the hope that they could be sent abroad for graduate training. From the early years, staff training was a major priority, counting on the enthusiastic support of the donor community. With the publication of the first strategic plan and receipt of considerable financial support from the World Bank and other major donors, staff training took a leap forward. The proportion of foreign teaching staff at the UEM dropped from 98 per cent in 1975 to only 14 per cent in the academic year 2000/01. Table 12

Table 12: Mozambican & foreign teaching staff, UEM

Year	Mozambican staff	Foreign staff	Total
1990/91	308 (67%)	149 (33%)	457
1991/2	466 (75%)	152 (25%)	618
1993/4	523 (77%)	124 (23%)	677
1994/5	470 (79%)	124 (21%)	594
1995/6	561 (81%)	137 (19%)	688
1996/7	585 (82%)	126 (18%)	711
2000/01	635 (86%)	100 (14%)	735

Sources: *Strategic Plan of Higher Education*; *Boletim Estatistico da UEM* (1991–2000).

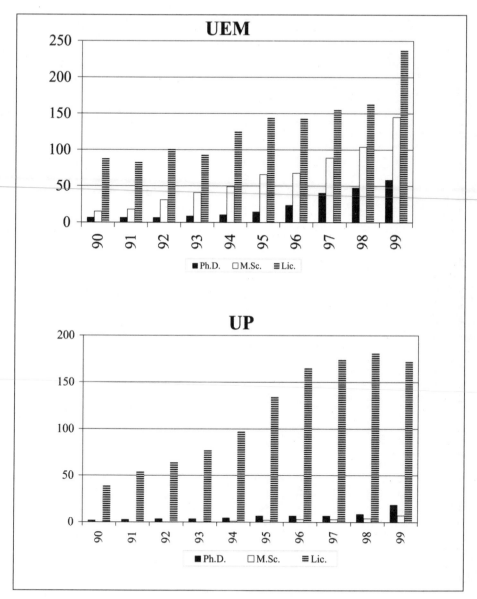

Figure 6: Academic staff qualifications at UEM & UP, 1990–99

Source: *Strategic Plan of Higher Education* (2000).

Table 13: Distribution of the teaching staff by institution, academic degree & nationality

	Governmental institutions															
	UEM				UP				ISRI				Total			
	FT	PT	FTE	Head count	FT	PT	FTE	Head count	FT	PT	Tot	Head count	FT	PT	FTE	Head count
Mozambican																
Ph.D.	59	10	64	69	19		19	19	3		3	3	81	10	86	91
M.Sc.	145	46	168	191	7		7	7	14	2	15	16	166	48	190	214
Licentiate	237	134	304	371	172	18	181	190	25	14	32	39	434	166	517	600
Bach.	4		4	4									4		4	4
Total	445	190	540	635	198	18	207	216	42	16	50	58	685	224	797	909
Expatriate																
Ph.D.	42	3	44	45	0	12	6	12					42	15	49.5	57
M.Sc.	20	1	21	21		1	1	1					20	2	21	22
Licentiate	19	15	27	34									19	15	26.5	34
Bach.																
Total	81	19	91	100	0	13	7	13	0	0	0	0	81	32	97	113
Total																
Ph.D.	101	13	108	114	19	12	25	31	3	0	3	3	123	25	135.5	148
M.Sc.	165	47	189	212	7	1	8	8	14	2	15	16	186	50	211	236
Licentiate	256	149	331	405	172	18	181	190	25	14	32	39	453	181	543.5	634
Bach.	4		4	4									4		4	4
Total	526	209	631	735	198	31	214	229	42	16	50	58	766	256	894	1,022

Table 13 cont.

Non-governmental institutions

	ISCTEM				ISPU				UCM				Total			
	FT	PT	FTE	Head count	FT	PT	FTE	Head count	FT	PT	Tot	Head count	FT	PT	FTE	Head count
Mozambican																
Ph.D.		1	1	1		5	3	5						6	3	6
M.Sc.					2	33	19	35	4			4	6	33	23	39
Licentiate		69	36	70	3	81	44	84	5	10	10	15	9	160	89	169
Bach.						1	1	1	3		3	3	3	1	4	4
Total	1	70	36	71	5	120	65	125	12	10	17	22	18	200	118	218
Expatriate																
Ph.D.	3	8	7	11	1	3	3	4	2	2	3	4	6	13	13	19
M.Sc.		1	1	1	2	5	5	7	9	7	13	16	11	13	18	24
Licentiate		27	14	27	6	13	13	19	10	15	18	25	16	55	44	71
Bach.									1	2	2	3	1	2	2	3
Total	3	36	21	39	9	21	20	30	22	26	35	48	34	83	76	117
Total																
Ph.D.	3	9	8	12	1	8	5	9	2	2	3	4	6	19	16	25
M.Sc.	0	1	1	1	4	38	23	42	13	7	17	20	17	46	40	63
Licentiate	1	96	49	97	9	94	56	103	15	25	28	40	25	215	133	240
Bach.					1	1	1	4	2	5	6	4	3	6	7	7
Total	4	106	57	110	14	141	85	155	34	36	52	70	52	283	194	335

details the increase in Mozambican staff over the years 1990–2001. As their numbers increased, the qualifications of Mozambican staff rose correspondingly (Figure 6).

After the introduction of non-governmental HEIs

With the growth in the number of HEIs, the total teaching staff reached 1,357 in 2000. Table 13 shows the way in which they are distributed throughout higher education, the numbers of full-time and part-time staff and the qualifications and nationalities of teachers. They are shown in terms of both the actual number of staff employed (the head count) and their full-time equivalents (FTE), assuming that two part-time teachers are the equivalent of one full-time teacher.

This table reveals a number of interesting comparisons. In the first place, the non-governmental institutions are more dependent on expatriate teaching staff than the governmental institutions, as Figure 7 demonstrates. This reflects their close links to the Portuguese university system and the fact that they are relatively new institutions.

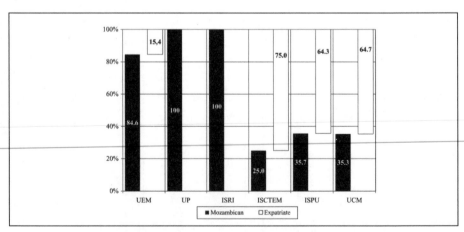

Figure 7: Mozambican & expatriate full-time teaching staff at HEIs
Source: *Strategic Plan of Higher Education* (2000).

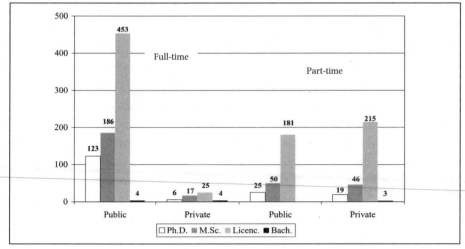

Figure 8: Educational qualifications of full-time & part-time teaching staff at HEIs

Source: *Strategic Plan of Higher Education* (2000).

Another significant difference between the governmental and non-governmental HEIs is that the former rely much less on part-time teaching staff than the latter, as Figure 8 shows. The data show that public institutions employ mainly full-time teachers, while private HEIs rely mainly on part-time staff, with the exception of UCM where the proportion of full-time and part-time teachers is almost 1:1. At ISCTEM and ISPU, the percentages of full-time teachers are only 3.6 and 9.0 per cent, respectively.

It should be emphasized that a large number of part-time teachers from private institutions (especially ISCTEM and ISPU) are also full-time teachers in the public institutions. They use employment in the private sector to supplement the low salary paid by public institutions. Many argue that this practice weakens the governmental institutions by reducing the time available for research and helping students. We tend to agree with this point but with reservations. According to official UEM annual reports, moonlighting has been a

41

customary practice for university teachers at least since the early 1990s. It may be preferable that these teachers moonlight in non-governmental HEIs rather than in other institutions with lesser social return. One could argue that the non-governmental institutions are providing what the government claims it cannot do, namely, the possibility of a salary of middle-class proportions for university teachers.

The problem may be perceived to lie elsewhere as we shall discuss later in this study. It is reputed that teachers who work in both kinds of university tend to teach 'better' in the non-governmental institutions, where their performance is closely monitored and evaluated by senior staff and the students themselves.

The rate at which Mozambicans have acquired postgraduate degrees and returned to take up teaching positions at Mozambican universities is testimony to the effectiveness of the training programmes developed to date. A shifting paradigm is already under way. Reflecting the changes in the political order in South Africa, dozens of Mozambicans have been and are enrolling increasingly in HEIs in South Africa for their master's degrees and doctorates. If the political situation stabilizes, study in Zimbabwe is also an attractive alternative to postgraduate training overseas. Postgraduate training in the region is much cheaper, and student exchange is an excellent way to promote cooperation amongst Southern Africa Development Community countries. This may also contribute to lessening the brain drain from the region to overseas countries.

5 Relevance, Quality, Quantity

What is taught, where & how

The undergraduate courses on offer in Mozambique in 2001 are presented in Table 14.

Table 14: Undergraduate courses on offer at HEIs, 2001

Governmental		Denominational			For-profit	
UEM	UP	ISRI	UCM	ISPU	ISCTEM	ISUTC
Natural Sciences						
Physics Chemistry Biology Geology						
Human & Social Sciences						
Social Sciences Anthro-pology Geography Linguistics History	Psychology & Pedagogy	International Relations	Education			
Engineering						
Chemical Electrical Civil Mechanical				Civil		Transport
Agriculture						
Farm engineering Rural engineering Forest engineering Crop production Vet. science		Agronomy				

Table 14 cont.

Liberal professions						
Law Medicine Architecture			Law Medicine Nursing	Law Psychology	Dentistry	
Business and Administration						
Economics Management			Economics	Management Accounting Administration Tourism	Management Accounting	Management
Information Sciences						
Computer science				Computer science Communication Sciences	Computer science Computer engineering	Computer & Telecom engineering
Teacher Training						
	Physical education Physics French Geography English Maths Maths & Physics Portuguese Chemistry Chemistry & Biology		History			
26	11	1	7	9	5	3

Source: University students' manuals.

The way we have classified university disciplines is not wholly traditional. Rather, it aims to relate course content to the world outside the university. The course offerings in themselves indicate important differences in the field. The UEM curriculum is clearly modelled on the classical European model with a balance between the arts, sciences and tech- nologies. The Catholic University seems to be aiming towards a similar classical model, but is more attuned to market considerations. ISRI is a rather isolated faculty, while the Pedagogical University is a teachers' training college. The three for-profit institutions – ISPU, ISCTEM and ISUTC – con- centrate on business, administration and information science and technology.

The simplest interpretation of these data is that the for-profit institutions try to maximize the market acceptability of the courses offered while minimizing the costs. Indeed, the labour market sector that offers the highest rewards to graduates is business administration, management and information tech- nology. These courses require little capital outlay (computer science may be an exception) and therefore offer a steady return on investment. ISCTEM started a course in dentistry, but is thinking of phasing it out, because of the considerable capital costs (for surgeries), high current expenditures (from the use of foreign lecturers) and small return from students' fees.

The state institutions can afford to be less dependent on market demand since they earn next to nothing from fees while lecturers' salaries are guaranteed by the state. Further- more, UEM sees itself as the bearer of university tradition in Mozambique, the mother of all the other institutions, and therefore the closest to the classical model.

From its inception, the Catholic University has developed in contrast to UEM. As we have seen, it was conceived as a regional counterpoint to the Maputo-based government institution as part of the process of reconciliation between FRELIMO and RENAMO when hostilities ended in October

1992. The choice to begin with faculties of law, economics and education was determined by the university's mentors, the Italian Bishops' Conference, who felt that these three areas were fundamental to the self-determination of the Mozambican people. The emphasis on education also came from Dom Manuel Vieira Pinto, formerly the Bishop of Nampula, an admirer of the teaching of Paulo Freire, who argued strongly for the importance of community-based education. This emphasis on community and service has guided curriculum development throughout the Catholic University. Thus, the course in agronomy in Cuamba concentrates on peasant and family farming systems and leans heavily on research and outreach within local farming communities. The course in medicine, which began in 2002, is being developed in collaboration with the University of Maastricht and will concentrate on teaching medicine deemed appropriate for the rural and urban poor of Mozambique. The curriculum will be problem-based. Thus, curriculum and teaching methods are in distinct contrast to the UEM Faculty of Medicine, which the Catholic University considers much more traditional.

Another important innovation at the Catholic University is the importance given to the teaching of English. At all the other HEIs, English is taught in a perfunctory manner. All UCM courses include English teaching, which can take up as much as half the curriculum in the first semesters, declining in quantity over subsequent ones. The university leadership argues that English is absolutely essential for graduates to be able to communicate with their English-speaking neighbours in Zimbabwe, Malawi, Tanzania, Swaziland and South Africa and to read international scientific literature.

Strategic planning

Strategic planning is a fairly recent phenomenon in Mozambican higher education institutions. UEM engaged in the first serious strategic planning effort in the early 1990s, culminating in the development of a plan that came to be known as *The Present and Perspectives* (UEM, 1991). This plan was later partially transformed into the Capacity Building Project funded by the World Bank. The project is currently winding down.

As follow-up to *The Present and Perspectives*, in 1997 the UEM rector appointed a committee to work out a five-year university strategic plan. This plan adopted a participatory approach, involving the entire university community and the stakeholders. A SWOT (Strengths, Weaknesses, Opportunities, Threats) analysis was undertaken to identify strengths, weaknesses and/or threats, after which vision and mission statements were drawn up and discussed, and guiding principles and key strategic issues identified. After a series of workshops within the university, the University Council approved 12 strategic objectives in October 1998.

The most important objectives dealt with reforming the academic, administrative and management structure and functioning of the university, with the aim of attaining:

- internal and external academic efficiency (improving the quality of education, increasing the graduation and intake rate, assuring regional, social and gender equity in access to higher education and improving the physical plant to meet the challenges of expansion);
- administrative and management efficiency (overcoming excessive centralization and bureaucracy in academic, administrative and financial management of the university and improving the management of human resources, as well as assuring more autonomy from the government and decentralization of certain activities to the faculties and departments);
- more efficiency in national and international cooperation;
- a culture of strategic planning in the management of the university.

This strategic plan was later put into operation and transformed into a project that is under discussion by the government and the World Bank.

In the meantime other governmental HEIs followed suit and started producing their own strategic plans. This trend gained more momentum when the Ministry of Education set up a committee in October 1999, composed of representatives of UEM, UP and ISRI, to work out a national strategic plan for higher education. The committee adopted the following methodology:

- gathering and analysis of documents and statistics on higher education in Mozambique as well as macroeconomic indicators of the country's economic performance and projections for 10–15 years;
- interviews with
  - (i) government officials;
  - (ii) the productive sector (both public and private);
  - (iii) civil society;
  - (iv) internal and external donors, funding agencies and institutions;
  - (v) non-governmental organizations (NGOs);
  - (vi) alumni.

Efficiency

All of the diagnoses of education in Mozambique since *The Present and Perspectives* have drawn attention to the high drop-out rate and the abnormally long time that students take to complete their undergraduate degrees at UEM.

The *Strategic Plan of Higher Education* is no exception to this rule. Calculating the rate of graduation by dividing the number of graduates by the number of students entering instruction five years earlier, the plan derived the following table for UEM and UP.

Table 15: Graduation rates in governmental HEIs, 1995–8 (%)

Year	UEM	UP	Total
1995	6.7	15.6	9.8
1996	7.6	14.9	9.3
1997	6.0	10.7	7.1
1998	6.6	11.3	7.7
Average	6.7	13.1	8.5

Source: *Strategic Plan of Higher Education* (2000).

Both UP and UEM have extremely low graduation rates, but that of UP is considerably better for reasons that are not clear. It may be that the UP does not insist upon a dissertation for the completion of the *licenciatura* degree. Because of their extreme youth there are no comparable figures for the non-governmental institutions. The Catholic University has graduated only two cohorts of students, both at bachelor's degree level. Of the 60 who began their bachelor's degree in economics, 23, or 43 per cent, passed. Of the 60 who began the course in education, 13, or 22 per cent passed. When we expressed our admiration to the leadership of the UCM, we were surprised to find that they did not share our pleasure. They intend to reduce the pass rates in the coming years, arguing that a high pass rate is indicative of low quality. Both ISPU and ISCTEM have produced their first graduates at bachelor's level. Graduation rates in these two for-profit HEIs, however, seem to follow two different directions. For instance, in 1999 and 2000, graduation rates at ISPU Maputo were 38 and 34 per cent, respectively; in 2000, the graduation rate at ISPU Quelimane was 30 per cent. By contrast, only 2, or 7.4 per cent, of the 27 students who attended the computer science programme at ISCTEM managed to complete their degree without having to repeat their courses.

All manner of remedies have been suggested for this chronic problem, ranging from curriculum reform to the introduction of new teaching techniques. Our opinion is that we are observing in Mozambique what in Brazil has been called the culture of repetition, whereby students are failed systematically throughout their educational careers. Change is possible only with a change in the academic culture as a whole that defines the attitudes of teachers and their students to the educational process. It is worth recalling the situation at UEM in the early 1980s when there were lecturers from over 27 different countries. These lecturers spoke different languages and brought different academic cultures with them. The Cubans acquired a reputation for passing over 90 per cent of their students. When the Mozambicans expressed their surprise, the Cubans retorted: 'We came to Mozambique to train Mozambican graduates, not to fail them.'

But available data suggest that the tendency of some students in high demand fields such as economics, management, law and engineering to take employment before completing the licentiate thesis is responsible for low graduation rates. We argue that this strengthens our point of view about the test of relevance being the ability to think creatively and flexibly and suggests that, to some extent, it has been achieved after four years of study without the need for a thesis. At the same time, since those students who do not return become part of graduation rate statistics, they inflate the apparent length of time taken to complete. From this perspective, leaving the university before completion could be regarded as synonymous with success (getting a job) rather than as dropping out.

Qualitative information gleaned from interviews with students, secondary schoolteachers and pedagogical directors at two non-governmental institutions suggests that part of the problem may be that the public universities, unlike the non-governmental HEIs, have no system for evaluating the performance of teachers. Non-governmental secondary schoolteachers to whom we spoke attributed the relative success of their schools to excellent teaching. When we pointed out that the majority of the teachers also teach in government schools, they responded that the same teachers teach better when they are paid well and evaluated regularly. They maintain that this holds true at university level as well. The non-governmental HEIs pay twice as much as the governmental HEIs but demand due dedication on the part of their employees. Teachers at ISCTEM, for example, are subjected to regular, anonymous student evaluations that determine whether their contracts will be renewed or not.

The data from our survey indicate that students are as critical of the learning environment as the writers of official reports. Less than 40 per cent of students at UEM were satisfied with the curriculum in comparison with almost 80 per cent for ISRI and 60 per cent for ISPU.

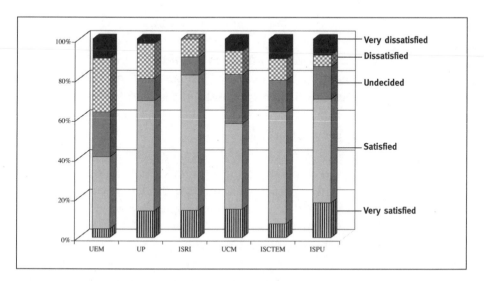

Figure 9: Students' satisfaction with curriculum

Source: Student survey.

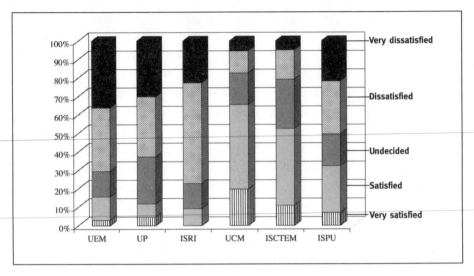

Figure 10: Students' satisfaction with books & learning environment

Source: Student survey.

In relation to books and the learning environment, the three non-governmental institutions outstrip the three governmental ones. Two-thirds (66 per cent) of UCM students, 52 per cent at ISCTEM and 32 per cent at ISPU declared themselves satisfied with books and the learning environment, as opposed to 15.6 per cent at UEM, 11.7 per cent at UP and only 9.1 per cent at ISRI.

In evaluating the quality and quantity of lecturers' attention to students and feedback, the picture is more complex. Only 26 per cent of UEM students said they were satisfied, while the corresponding figures were 38.6 per cent at UCM, 50 per cent at ISRI, 52 per cent at UP, 53 per cent at ISPU and 55 per cent at ISCTEM.

These data suggest that while the dissatisfaction of students is widespread, it is greater at UEM than at other governmental and non-governmental institutions. It is difficult to interpret this difference. It is likely, however, that these opinions reflect

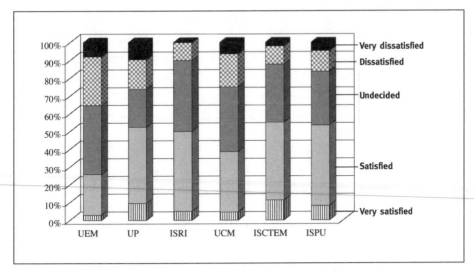

Figure 11: Students' satisfaction with quantity & quality of lecturers' attention & feedback

Source: Student survey.

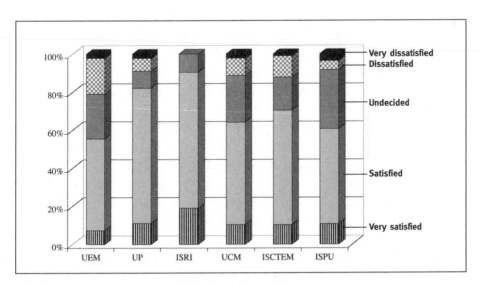

Figure 12: Students' intellectual development satisfaction

Source: Student survey.

53

the fact that UEM teachers spend less time with their UEM students than at their other activities, including teaching at non-governmental institutions. The higher rating of UP may have to do with lower expectations in the first place, while at ISRI it may well be related to the extremely favourable staff/student ratio and to the fact that all students follow the same course.

It is also possible, of course, that the students' satisfaction is based to a large extent on the degree to which they see their university experience as equipping them for a successful professional life. It could be argued, therefore, that from the point of the students at ISRI, UP, ISCTEM, UCM and ISPU, their courses prepare them more adequately for their future careers. To test this hypothesis it would be necessary to look at the degree of student satisfaction with different careers at UEM.

Relevance

Throughout the strategic plans of UEM and the Ministry of Higher Education, there is a demand that courses be relevant either by preparing students for specific niches within the rapidly changing labour market or by producing graduates imbued with the idea of service to their country.

However, in our brief interviews with the two major employment agencies in Maputo (MOZAL and Ports and Railways) we were dismayed to learn that course content and particular faculties or universities are of little interest to potential employers. What they are looking for, they claimed, are people with a certain attitude or work ethic. True to the imperatives of the 'new economy', what interests employers much more than substantive knowledge is the ability to think and act with flexibility and creativity. The employment agents to whom we spoke were adamant that such qualities were 'innate' and were spread evenly across the Mozambican academic board. These are sobering thoughts to those of us who believe in the transforming power of education!

The fact is that Mozambique offers a wide spectrum of undergraduate degrees, the content of which is probably nearer to market demand that one might have thought. Even if there is not a completely tight fit between courses and market, this does not seem to be the problem that might be assumed at first sight. However, we must stress the need for curriculum reform, especially at UEM, which is under way. Old-fashioned programmes, based on the rote transfer of encyclopaedic knowledge by omniscient professors slow to react to social changes and a labour market that demands flexibility and creativity, are extremely expensive and mammoth-like.

Indeed, a key element of the ongoing curriculum reform at UEM is the replacement of the old five-year *licenciatura* degree by a three-year bachelor's or four-year *licenciatura* degree. In turn, such structural changes, while paving the way for introducing master's degrees and doctorates, can be regarded as the solid foundation of UEM's role as the Mecca, if not the mother, of research and graduate study in Mozambique.

Efforts to improve efficiency & relevance

BUSCEP at UEM

The purpose of the Basic Science University Programme (BUSCEP) was to provide students entering the university with the basic skills and attitudes that they did not acquire in secondary school and help them make a smooth transition into higher education. Realizing that the level of secondary-school leavers in mathematics and science was unsatisfactory as a basis for further academic studies, UEM decided to introduce a remedial or bridging course for first-year students in science and mathematics-based subjects. This was developed in collaboration with the Free University of Amsterdam (FUA), with financial support from the Netherlands Directorate General for International Cooperation (DGIS). It started as a pilot project with an 18-week course for 75 agronomy students in 1986. By 1989 it had expanded to 338 students in agronomy, biology, engineering and science. During the expansion phase the European Union provided additional support. In 1992 the total number of weeks dedicated to the basic science programme was reduced to 16, although its content remained unchanged.

An external evaluation of the programme conducted in 1997 concluded that despite having failed to meet some of its initial objectives, BUSCEP had been a successful project. The programme was fully integrated and widely supported within the university and, consequently, was sustainable. A number of people, however, did not subscribe to these views. During the preparatory phase of the ongoing curriculum reform the Central Commission for Curriculum Reform (CCRC) at UEM conducted a survey with deans, heads of department, faculty members and students to assess the impact of BUSCEP on the quality of the teaching and learning process. The CCRC concluded that the basic semester did not manage to raise the knowledge levels of the students because of the fast deterioration of the teaching and learning environment in Mozambican secondary schools, the lack of integration into, and support of, secondary school-teachers for the BUSCEP programme and the poor connection and collaboration between faculties at the receiving end and BUSCEP.

However, they also cautioned that the quality of the teaching and students' profiles in different study programmes did not depend only on the basic semester but also on the teaching methods used in the basic subjects of each programme, particularly during the first two years of the curriculum.

Zero semesters & propaedeutic years

The non-governmental universities adopted a more radical stance in relation to the quality of their first-year students than the governmental universities. While UEM instituted BUSCEP courses for natural science, engineering and agriculture students, ISPU, ISCTEM, ISUTC and the UCM instituted what the first three call a 'zero semester' and what the UCM calls a propaedeutic year, with no entrance examination necessary. Students with a solid secondary-school education pass directly to the full university course. Those with more problems follow the zero or propaedeutic year prior to sitting the entrance exams.

Another innovation to try to improve graduation rates has been to move away from the five-year licentiate which had been the norm since 1985, following the adoption of the five-year degree plus thesis model that was used in the former Soviet Union, in East Germany and in Portugal, towards a three-year bachelor degree. Thereafter students may either leave the university or, in the case of those with higher grades, continue to master's or licentiate degrees.

The rector of UCM believes that the university should provide degrees that are successively more difficult to obtain. Those who pass at bachelor's level, for example, would move directly into the labour market. Those who complete their *licenciatura* would move into positions requiring higher qualifications, while those who continue to master's or doctorate level would be natural candidates for joining the university faculty, equipped to train future generations.

Curriculum reform at UEM

The reflections and debates surrounding the initial phase of the ongoing curriculum reform at UEM allow one to elaborate a picture of the present situation as follows:

• graduation rates are too low compared with the rates of

57

other universities in the region and the rest of the world;
- a five-year training programme is too long and onerous for a limited state budget, which supports the largest share of educational expenditure;
- with the exception of the Faculty of Social Sciences (UFICS), most programmes are based on a single-stage structure (a five-year *licenciatura* without any intermediate stage);
- in addition to being too long, the present curricula are encyclopaedic and reflect a compartmentalized and static view of knowledge;
- by and large the existing study plans are characterized by very heavy course loads that in certain cases go beyond 32 hours per week;
- most programmes have a rigid prerequisite system that conditions student graduation to the preparation of a *licenciatura* thesis;
- the professional and graduate profiles of the existing programmes are outdated and irrelevant to the needs of Mozambican society.

Under these circumstances, the purpose of curriculum reform was to adjust the existing curricula to the needs of Mozambican society in general, and the labour market in particular, to produce the quantity and quality of workforce needed for social and economic development. Steps designed to increase graduation rates within the university include the reduction of the length of the study programmes from five to four years, as well as the possibility of introducing three-year bachelor degrees, where appropriate. A reduction in the number of contact hours from 32 to 20–25 hours a week was also recommended. Measures designed to boost quality and efficiency and stimulate lifelong learning include:

- introduction of postgraduate training (specialist diplomas and master's degrees) in the academic year 2001/02;

- equipping and improving libraries and computer labs;
- providing the teaching staff, particularly junior lecturers, with opportunities for postgraduate training and professional development.

The following measures are advocated to improve the relevance of the curricula:

- clearly defining the professional and graduate profiles of each programme, based on an analysis of the needs of the society and the labour market;
- improving the admission system to the university through the development of more valid and reliable instruments of student assessment;
- promoting a closer link between teaching and research through applied research;
- introducing of postgraduate training.

6 Information & Communication Technologies: Policies and Use

The Informatics Centre of Eduardo Mondlane University (CIUEM) has been at the forefront of internet activities in Mozambique since the early 1990s when it began to offer nationwide e-mail services. In 1996 Mozambique became the second country in sub-Saharan Africa outside South Africa to achieve full internet connectivity through a dial-up connection between CIUEM and Rhodes University in South Africa. Although there are now several commercial Internet Service Providers in Mozambique, UEM remains at the forefront of internet development and information society initiatives in the country.[1] In the area of ICT, UEM is also well in advance of Mozambique's other universities, both governmental and non-governmental. This is in large part due to the university's leadership, which has been strongly supportive of and knowledgeable about ICT implementation. UEM has also received considerable donor funding for its ICT initiatives. In view of UEM's pre-eminent role in ICT and because our information is most complete for it, the bulk of this chapter will focus on ICT at UEM. Nevertheless, wherever possible we shall cover Mozambique as a whole in the following areas: strategic planning; utilization of ICT in faculties and departments; and library and documentation services.

ICT at UEM

ICT strategic planning and implementation

If pictures really do speak louder than words, then ICT figures prominently in the university's thinking, as evidenced by the latest version of the *Strategic Plan*, which contains a full-page ad with photos and text for CIUEM on the flyleaf. No other unit within the university receives such prominence in the plan. Computers figure prominently in the remaining photographs, as well; four out of 21 photographs show people doing things with computers (or next to them) – including the photograph at the top of strategic objective 11 'to promote and publicize the university's image'.

The plan presents a number of recommendations in order to make UEM a more effective institution. ICT is mentioned in several places, most notably in strategic objectives on administration and management; excellence and quality; and on increasing admission rates. The ICT recommendations range from the most mundane, such as equipping systems with a 'telephone (including fax), computer or radio where applicable', to ensuring that all of the libraries are fully computerized and internet-accessible, that ICT training is offered to all members of the university and that distance education for undergraduate and postgraduate students is implemented. The *Strategic Plan*, however, gives no concrete guidelines on achieving these objectives.

A university-wide two-day workshop was held in April 2000 to prepare a new ICT policy plan for the university. Representatives of every faculty, department and unit participated. Issues covered during the workshop included presentations on the situation at UEM vis-à-vis ICT, ICT applications and policy issues. On the policy side, the discussion focused on these questions.

- Who is responsible for procurement, and how is it done?
- How should hardware and software standards be defined and by whom?
- Who is responsible for the backbone?
- Who is responsible for the university's gateway to the internet?
- Who is responsible for the Local Area Networks (LANs)?
- Who is responsible for the university's management information systems (MIS) and the library information system (LIS)?
- On finance and budget questions, who pays for technical assistance? Where does the maintenance budget go? What

61

should be included in the university's ICT budget policy? How can faculties and units contribute to pay for the backbone and other common costs?

The workshop was meant to raise questions, not to answer them. CIUEM will use input from the workshop in drafting its ICT policy plan.

Perhaps because UEM has shown itself to be so receptive to ICT planning and implementation, it has been able to garner considerable donor support – from the Dutch, the Swedes and the World Bank. In addition, private foundations, such as the Ford Foundation, have supported ICT for their grantees, some examples of which are given in the section on ICT implementation in selected faculties and centres.

With funding from the World Bank Capacity-Building Project, the Government of the Netherlands and SIDA/SAREC, the university is in the process of creating the Eduardo Mondlane University Network (EMUNet).[2] When fully in place, EMUNet will consist of:

- a fibre-optic backbone to all buildings on the main campus;
- wireless links from off-campus sites to the backbone, including the administration building, faculties of architecture, engineering, veterinary medicine, medicine, law, the Natural History Museum, the Historical Archive and a few other sites;
- LANs, network points and small computer labs in each of the university's faculties, units, or centres.

It was expected that by the end of 2001, the campus backbone would be fully in place and each building would have the requisite infrastructure. In addition, UEM was planning to upgrade its VSAT bandwidth.[3]

When this study was carried out in June 2001, it was generally acknowledged that the current situation was far from satisfactory. Cable was just being laid for the backbone. The rector's lodging was the only building hooked up to CIUEM via a wireless link. With the exception of this and CIUEM, dial-up connections were necessary to access the internet. Using the CIUEM connection was considered so slow that some users opted for commercial service providers. CIUEM and the university as a whole were under pressure to provide better internet services. Since then, progress has been made in networking the campus and in speeding up access to the internet.

Another frustration now being rectified is the inadequate bandwidth. Until very recently it was difficult to access the UEM's home page because it loaded up so slowly. The UEM website is a particularly good one, which includes, among other things, a Portuguese-language guide to the internet.[4] More bandwidth has since been installed, with SIDA/SAREC funding, which has improved loading times.

Like many other African universities, UEM is grappling with ICT applications for teaching, learning and research. Some departments and faculties – most notably agriculture and medicine – have moved forward on their own initiative to utilize ICT more effectively. In addition, the university's Staff Development Project (STADEP) is working with faculty to help them use ICT in their teaching. Improving the capacity of the university community to use ICT is also a major component of support from the Netherlands government.

ICT at the university is also noteworthy because UEM sees itself within a broader perspective than the confines of the university. With funding from the International Development Research Centre of Canada (IDRC), UEM is actively engaged in community outreach programmes through IDRC's Acacia Initiative. CIUEM staff are responsible for the implementation of two IDRC-funded community telecentres close to Maputo (at Namaacha and Manhica) and for the Kellogg Foundation-supported telecentre in Manica Province.[5] In addition, the

63

university is working with the government commission headed by the Prime Minister to establish a national information policy.[6] UEM is unique among African universities in the depth of its commitment to helping set up national ICT policies and to promoting community access to ICT.

Utilization of ICT in faculties & departments

UEM staff identified agronomy, architecture, engineering and medicine as the strongest faculties in ICT implementation. The ICT situation at the agronomy and medicine faculties and at STADEP is detailed below.

Agronomy

The Faculty of Agronomy is devoting considerable attention to improving access to information for staff and students, but a range of problems still needs to be addressed.

- Structural damage forced the faculty to close its library and move the books that were not ruined to another location.
- The library has few books and journal subscriptions.
- The internet was not yet available, except through dial-up connections.
- Language is a serious issue since many students and some lecturers cannot read technical English.
- There are not enough computers for faculty, students and staff.

To ameliorate these problems, the following actions have been taken.[7]

- The library is being reconstructed and renovated, as is the entire Faculty of Agronomy. The renovated library was scheduled to reopen in 2001.
- A part-time librarian was engaged for the faculty library and is making recommendations to the faculty on acquisitions.

- The faculty received Portuguese funding to acquire *The Essential Electronic Agricultural Library* (TEEAL) on CD-ROM, a collection of 100 full-text agricultural journals. It has also received a donation of *TROPAG & RURAL* and plans to establish a collection of key reference books.
- The faculty is improving its computing capability. In April 2000 there were only 20 computers for use by the students, and the computer room was very crowded. Twenty more computers will be purchased – two for the library and the remainder for a new, networked computer lab. The older computers will be used for word processing and other functions that do not require much capacity. The new machines will be loaded with statistical packages, irrigation software and GIS.

Medicine

The Faculty of Medicine, including its library, is also being renovated. There is a computer lab with 12 computers. Although the room is small, there are plans to add another 36 PCs. There will also be a second computer room for literature searches (both CD-ROM and internet) after the library is finished. Maintenance and upgrading remain problem areas, however.

The faculty maintains an e-mail server with over 500 mailboxes for students and staff. In the beginning e-mail was totally free; now a token payment of 5,000 *meticais* (about US$0.25) a month is assessed. With funding from the World Bank, there are plans to develop a faculty network and internet links to the affiliated teaching hospital and four district hospitals (Niassa, Gaza, Inhambane and Maputo) where the students go on rotation. As there are already e-mail links to the districts, the advent of an internet connection would make a modified form of telemedicine possible.

The Faculty of Medicine is also working on a health information system project, funded by NORAD, which began

65

in South Africa. The aim is to change the way health information is gathered. A pilot project is under way in the four districts listed above.

The application of ICT to teaching and learning is also of concern to the faculty. The Orient Foundation has offered a three-month course on digital libraries. Students taking biochemistry are expected to present their projects on a home page, and physiology is to follow suit. Groups of students gather information and transfer their reports to a home page. They are then judged according to the quality of the information itself, links and graphics. The aim is to help the students understand that there are different ways to convey information, but the problem is that there is no follow-up, so that students can easily forget the web development skills that they learn.

In general, training is considered a critical issue for students and staff alike – learning how to use computers, databases, e-mail and internet. STADEP organized a short course on the internet for paediatrics staff from the faculty and the Central Hospital of Maputo, which covered internet basics, how to find biomedical/scientific information on the internet and how to use *Medline*. A similar course was offered for public health practitioners.

The faculty offers students a two-semester elective course on informatics. During the first semester they learn basic computer literacy. During the second, they learn standard applications (spreadsheets, word processing and a database). In the second year of studies 'Introduction to Research Methodologies' is offered, which teaches students how to do literature searches on CD-ROM and the internet.[8]

Centre for Academic Development (CAD)
STADEP was established with Netherlands funding in 1989 to help academic staff improve the quality of their teaching. STADEP has now become the Centre for Academic Develop-

ment, housed in the Faculty of Education, and will now begin to work with students as well. There is also some interest in expanding the Centre beyond the confines of UEM and offering services to other Mozambican universities. One problem that the Centre faces, however, is a shortage of staff. With only five people on the staff, it is difficult to contemplate much expansion.

The use of ICT in education is a new area for the Centre. Initial training courses in this area comprise: providing skills in the use of software, particularly Powerpoint, and use of the internet. The internet course is taught in collaboration with CIUEM. Teaching staff from all parts of the university take this course. In addition, some faculties, such as medicine, have requested special internet courses focusing on their discipline.

In October 2000, STADEP convened an ICT workshop for the Faculty of Education, with the following objectives:

- to build awareness of the importance of ICT in education;
- to discuss the role of ICT in curriculum development;
- to identify ways for teachers and students to use ICT in the faculty.

Following this initial workshop, the Centre has been charged with conducting similar workshops for other faculties and units at UEM.[9]

Directorate for Documentation Services (DDS)
UEM has no central library; rather there are 17 separate faculty and departmental libraries, located on each of the university's campuses.[10] Some of these libraries, such as the one at the Centre for African Studies, fulfil their objectives admirably, while others suffer from poor infrastructure, not enough room and insufficient resources in general.

The university is further hampered in its ability to provide good library services because there are so few trained librarians on its staff. At independence, the only trained librarians at the university all returned to Portugal, leaving behind a Mozambican staff with minimal educational skills (11 years of schooling) and no training in library management. As late as 1992 there were only 11 or 12 people in the entire country with university degrees in library science.

To compound the problem, there has never been a school of library science in Mozambique.[11] UEM has had to send staff abroad for training – most typically to Botswana for those staff who speak English, or to Brazil. This provides a good nucleus, but there are still not enough librarians to meet the need. The fact that faculty/departmental libraries are so dispersed intensifies the problem. In addition, it may be difficult to retain these newly-trained librarians. With the growth of the internet in Mozambique, there is an increased demand for information professionals in the private sector and in international organizations.[12]

To date, none of the libraries is totally computerized. In the early 1990s, UNDP gave the Faculty of Economics a grant of $556,000 to upgrade library services, to create a computerized database using the Portuguese equivalent of CDS/ISIS and to train staff.[13] The project was constrained by lack of computers and not enough trained staff.

The DDS now has funding from the Netherlands government to purchase an appropriate library information system package and to train staff, and from SIDA/SAREC to acquire computers and other equipment. In the meantime, staff have begun to create bibliographic databases using WINISIS, the Windows version of CDS/ISIS, working on stand-alone computers. They are starting first with DDS holdings and then plan to move on to other UEM libraries.

Records are entered manually as a start. Inputters receive 5,000 *meticais* (about US$0.25) for each record created. They are then entered into the computer database, at a price of

2,000 *meticais* for each record. As of April 2000, about 5,000 records had been entered, but some of them were entered incorrectly and needed correction Moreover, the entries were made without subject headings or keywords.

Selecting a library information system (LIS) software package has not been without its vicissitudes. In 1999 the university received Ford Foundation funding to permit two librarians to visit Johannesburg and Cape Town to observe the computerization of GAELIC and CALICO, South Africa's two regional library consortia. A Dutch library consultant is working with UEM library staff to select the most appropriate and affordable LIS package.[14] Whichever library package is selected, two critical criteria are: that the package must be available in Portuguese; and bearing in mind that some staff are not technically sophisticated and have limited education, it must be simple to use.

In addition to funding for training and hardware acquisitions, SIDA/SAREC has been a key donor in support of UEM's library accessions budget, supplemented by a grant from the Ford Foundation for the Centre for African Studies.

DDS and library services in general are at a crossroads:

- more trained staff are in place, but numbers are insufficient to meet growing demands on the system;
- attempts at computerization are getting under way, but major decisions remain to be made;
- the library recently installed a networked internet café, with nine donated microcomputers. It must now begin to offer appropriate services to UEM students and staff;
- everyone at the university is convinced that a central library is desirable, but the effect this will have on the many small faculty and departmental libraries, not to mention the Historical Archive and other units loosely affiliated with UEM, has not been assessed.

69

Other governmental universities

Pedagogical University

Overall, UP appears to be the least well-resourced HEI in the area of ICT. This reflects its status as the poor relation of higher education, as mentioned earlier in this study. There are some computers and internet access in different departments on all of the campuses. The following is the overall situation.

- With funding from the Camões Institute, UP in Maputo opened an attractive Portuguese-language and literature library, which includes a multimedia computer and a link to the internet.

- The Faculty of Social Sciences in Maputo has a resource room with three computers, one of which has a dial-up connection to the internet, but the line is frequently down. Teachers can log on and establish e-mail accounts. In the building where the Faculty of Social Sciences is located, there are only two e-mail access points for staff – one in Social Sciences and a second in the French department. In the Faculty of Natural Sciences, which is located in another building in Maputo, the internet connection is situated in the offices of the heads of departments, so access is very limited. Despite these difficulties, some members of the teaching staff recognize the need to use e-mail and the internet and encourage students in this direction. It is possible that if UP had better infrastructure and more equipment, there would be more enthusiasm for using ICT.

- The Beira campus has computers, purchased primarily through project support. SIDA/SAREC funded the computer lab's printer and ten computers, only five of which are working. The maths department has six microcomputers as part of an ethnomathematics project, but some are old and obsolete. The geography department has two PCs while the physics department has none. The Beira campus has a Teledata internet account.[15] Some lecturers also have private accounts of their own.

• In Nampula, UP has one computer with a dial-up connection to the internet using Teledata, which is used by many teachers.

Higher Institute for International Relations

The Higher Institute for International Relations (ISRI) is located in two different buildings in Maputo.[16] There are about 12 computers in the main ISRI building, all networked, and a few more in the second building. ISRI has a dial-up connection to the internet. The Rector uses the UEM system; the rest of ISRI is on Vircon, a private server in Maputo. Instructors have access to two internet-accessible computers; students can use the eight PCs in the computer lab or the computer in the library. ISRI wants to upgrade the system to a dedicated line, but as of now funding is insufficient.

ISRI has a small library, which was set up by the Centre for Brazilian Studies. There are two librarians, neither of whom have library diplomas or degrees. They are using WINISIS to catalogue the collection. One of the librarians did a computer course at UEM and a course on CDS/ISIS in the Netherlands. The library computer has a dial-up connection to the internet, which students can use.

ICT problems that staff mentioned include insufficient funding to acquire good internet access, more computers and maintaining the infrastructure, and lack of trained staff to service the computers or networks.

Non-governmental universities

The Catholic University

The Catholic University (UCM) ranks below UEM but above the rest of Mozambique's universities in terms of ICT facilities, except in the overall area of e-mail and internet access.

- E-mail and internet at UCM are restricted to dial-up connections. Each campus has a Teledata account; a few departments, such as CDDI, have their own accounts. Originally, UCM had hoped to be a major player in UNDP's Sustainable Development Networking Programme (SDNP) in Mozambique. The SDNP Mozambique coordinator asked UCM whether it would like to be a hub for Beira and receive a VSAT system. The project would also have funded some networking development on the Beira campus and a year of connectivity. The university agreed, and plans were set in motion. However, another consultant visited Mozambique and recommended that the VSAT be placed at the public telecommunications operator, Mozambique Telecommunications (TDM), instead. TDM received the VSAT, but does not appear to have done anything with it. The VSAT is not operational, and SDNP funding has run out.[17]

  The Beira campus of UCM has a computer lab, with ten networked computers. Although the computers are fairly new, their capacity is low – 16MB of RAM and 1.5GB hard drives. There are also computer labs in the faculties of law and education in Nampula.

- Each of the UCM libraries has a computer running Winnebago Spectrum library software with modules for cataloguing, circulation, users and materials. Winnebago was selected with the advice of the United States Information Service (USIS) in Maputo and funded by a grant from the Netherlands government.[18] The USIS librarian also helped set up the database.

- The library computers came equipped with six-disc CD-ROM drives. The Beira library has a few CD-ROMs.

- With funding from the Austrian government, UCM has installed a sophisticated Geographic Information System (GIS) laboratory within the Centre for Investigation and Documentation for Integrated Development (CDDI) on the Beira campus. There are six networked computers. The system was installed in November 1998 and has been extensively used, particularly during and after the February 2000 floods to integrate coordinates for relief efforts. Austrian support for this initiative includes the provision of equipment and training.

- In August 2000, UCM opened a Faculty of Biomedical Sciences on the Beira campus. The faculty's problem-based, patient-oriented approach requires the availability of a well-equipped resource centre. UCM recently submitted a request to the Netherlands Embassy to provide partial funding for the resource centre. The US$75,000 proposal included the purchase of equipment, multimedia CD-ROMs and basic textbooks.

The Catholic University has vision and recognizes the importance of ICT to its mission, but lacks the human resource base to use technology effectively. Up to now the university has depended on visiting scholars, clerical and secular, to provide know-how. The university librarians need both computer skills and librarianship training. Both university administrators and teaching staff recognize the problem.

ISPU

The Instituto Superior Politécnico e Universitário (ISPU) offers a number of degrees in the social sciences and technical subjects, including one in computer sciences, which allows for a major in either administration or telecommunications and new technologies.[19]

The Maputo campus is well equipped in terms of information technology equipment. It has a LAN and a leased line to Teledata for internet. There is one computer lab with ten PCs and a second multimedia lab with 15 computers, speakers, video equipment and an LCD projector. Students generally log on to the internet through Teledata and use free e-mail accounts. Internet services are free for students at ISPU. There are also three computers in the library. Lecturers sometimes ask their students to use the internet on homework assignments.

The library has computerized its holdings using Access software, and the database is available online through the ISPU website.[20] The library collection is small; it has no scholarly journals. However, its collection of textbooks and reference books is probably adequate for its needs. The ISPU library is hampered, however, by donations, an affliction not unknown to other African universities. Many of the books appear to be gifts from the Polytechnic of Macau, with which ISPU has an exchange programme. There are many Cantonese and Mandarin language tapes, for example, as well as stunning art books.

The Quelimane campus uses computers for the library and for administration, with the same software as used at the Maputo home base and links to the internet through Teledata. The Quelimane campus depends on teachers from Maputo offering course modules lasting for one or two months. Students send their essays to Maputo, where they are corrected and returned much later. Staff recognize that a consolidated e-mail system would facilitate this experiment in distance learning, not dissimilar to that used by the Nampula branch of the Pedagogical University. We were informed that the Ministry of the Environment is about to get an antenna from UEM that would be installed in Quelimane to service government departments and the ISPU campus. It could be used for an e-mail system.

ISCTEM & ISUTC

ISCTEM runs courses in computer engineering and maintains an excellent laboratory with 30 networked computers. The library is fully computerized, and there is considerable awareness of the importance of ICT. ISUTC took in its first 'zero year' students in 2000 and plans to specialize in computer studies with applications throughout the engineering subjects.

What do students say?

The survey document discussed earlier in this study included questions on e-mail and the internet, the availability of computers and library services.

Students were asked to prioritize a range of options in order to improve library services. In general, students at all the universities were unhappy with the functioning of their libraries.

In terms of library infrastructure, almost all the students surveyed put making 'photocopying facilities available to students at an affordable price' as their first priority. The numbers ranged from a high of over 70 per cent at UEM, ISCTEM and ISRI to a low of 52 per cent at UP. No other library-related question ranked as high in importance to the students who completed questionnaires. Other questions involved extending opening hours; at least 70 per cent of the students in the six universities put longer hours as either their first or second priority. Increasing seating capacity received similar responses, as did bibliographic control questions – allowing students to locate, access and borrow books more efficiently, for example. Almost unamimously students said

75

Table 16: Students' priorities on increasing library holdings (%)

	UEM	UP	ISRI	UCM	ISCTEM	ISPU
Ranking as 1st priority	82.8	79.1	85.7	72.1	68.6	84.7
Ranking as 2nd priority	10.1	14.0	14.3	16.4	18.6	7.1
Ranking as 3rd priority	5.0	2.3	0.0	5.5	8.1	3.5
Ranking as 4th priority	2.1	4.7	0.0	6.0	4.7	4.7

Source: Student survey.

that they wanted their universities to increase the number of books and journals purchased.

They would also like to have more copies of textbooks. Between 80 and 90 per cent of all students questioned put more copies as their first or second priority. Almost all the students wanted more Portuguese-language titles. ISRI and UCM were the only universities at which the majority of students wanted more English-language books and journals.

More students log on to e-mail and the internet than would have been expected, although, predictably, the numbers are greater at ISCTEM, ISPU and UEM than at the three other universities.

The fact that ISCTEM and ISPU have larger numbers of internet users than UEM is due to the fact that these universities currently have more technology at the disposal of their students than UEM. However, it could also reflect the higher socio-economic status of these students. Once the UEM campus backbone is in place and student computer labs installed, students at Mozambique's first university to implement the internet will have better access.

Table 17: Students using the internet (%)

Answer	UEM	UP	ISRI	UCM	ISCTEM	ISPU
Yes	52.2	4.3	34.8	15.9	63.5	56.5
No	46.6	93.6	60.9	74.7	34.6	41.3
No response	1.2	2.1	4.3	9.4	1.9	2.2

Source: Student survey.

Students send and receive e-mail from a variety of locations. At UEM they primarily use the computer lab. At ISRI they go to the library, where the internet computer is located. At the Catholic University, they access e-mail mainly from their homes or place of employment; very few use the campus facilities. At ISCTEM they use the computer lab or have access at home. ISPU students send e-mail from their home, the library, or their place of work. So few students use e-mail at UP that their responses were negligible and have not been factored into the discussion below.

Over 50 per cent of ISCTEM's students use e-mail at least once a week; 25 per cent of them reported that they log on every day, and 38 per cent are weekly users. At ISPU, the numbers are a little lower, but still more than 50 per cent are regular users on a daily or weekly basis. Almost half of the UEM students log on to e-mail at least once a week or more often. The numbers are lower at ISRI and the remaining universities. And, just like all of us, most of the students use e-mail to keep in touch with friends and families. Interestingly, fewer than 50 per cent of the students at UEM, ISRI and UCM appear to use internet for anything other than e-mail. ISCTEM and ISPU were the only ones to report significant online searching, and most of their students said that they were using the internet for research purposes.

The survey asked whether the students were familiar with

Table 18: Familiarity with computers before entering university (%)

Response	UEM	UP	ISRI	UCM	ISCTEM	ISPU
Very familiar	9.6	6.4	4.3	12.9	23.1	16.3
Sufficiently familiar	24.9	10.6	26.1	30.5	42.3	41.3
Slightly familiar	26.6	21.3	17.4	25.3	24.0	34.8
Not computer-literate	38.3	59.6	43.5	22.7	7.7	4.3
No response	0.7	2.1	8.7	8.6	2.9	3.3

Source: Student survey.

Table 19: Computer training in faculty (%)

Response	UEM	UP	ISRI	UCM	ISCTEM	ISPU
Yes	60.9	10.6	60.9	85.4	51.9	78.3
No	36.9	85.1	30.4	6.0	45.2	17.4
No response	2.1	4.3	8.7	8.6	2.9	4.3

Source: Student survey.

Table 20: Faculty requirements for students to use computers (%)

Response	UEM	UP	ISRI	UCM	ISCTEM	ISPU
Yes	49.0	19.1	43.5	63.5	36.5	30.4
No	36.9	46.8	39.1	19.7	37.5	41.3
Don't know	18.1	29.8	8.7	7.3	20.2	25.0
No response	1.4	4.3	8.7	9.4	5.8	3.3

Source: Student survey.

computers before they entered university, whether they received computer training in their faculties, and whether they were required to use computers for their university work.

With the exception of UP, at least half of the students entering university had some computer literacy – with ISCTEM in the lead, followed by ISPU, UCM, UEM and ISRI. Remarkably, considering the ICT infrastructure and capacity at UCM, students there are more likely to receive computer training. In fact, more than 50 per cent of the students at every university, except for UP, are given some computer training. Interestingly, students are not required to use these computer skills once they have them – the Catholic University is the only one of the six universities surveyed to require a large proportion of students to make use of computers, followed by UEM, ISRI, ISCTEM, ISPU and UP in that order. These low demands on students at ISPU and ISCTEM are puzzling in light of the fact that students at these two institutions are so well endowed with infrastructure and training. Equally perplexing is the fact that so many students at the six universities do not know whether their faculties require them to use computers in their work.

In sum, students at the Pedagogical University are the most severely disadvantaged in terms of ICT utilization. They do not have ready access to technology, they are not computer-literate when they enter university and few of them receive any training during their university years. Secondly, not surprisingly, students at ISPU and ISCTEM are reaping the rewards of a better infrastructure. In addition, they are more likely to be computer-literate before beginning university. Finally, despite the forward-looking ICT planning and policies at Eduardo Mondlane University, students there are not yet making full use of the technology. UEM is the best of the public universities in the area of ICT applications, but at the student level it falls far short of ISPU, ISCTEM and, in some ways, the Catholic University.

United States Agency for International Development (USAID)

USAID is implementing two activities in Mozambique with ICT ramifications. The first is the Leland Initiative, which provided a VSAT system that is used by several servers in the country. Recently the Education and Democracy for Development Initiative (EDDI) for Mozambique has provided funding to set up servers in Beira, Nampula, Quelimane, Chokwe and Cuamba, with subsidized broadband capability to selected institutions for one year. The Catholic University will receive a 64kbps line; the Pedagogical University is likely to receive a 33.6kbps line. It is possible that other institutions will qualify as well, including secondary schools that already have computer capability. It is important to remember, however, that this funding does not include the purchase of equipment or the installation of LANs. Moreover, after one year, the recipient institutions will have to support this internet access themselves. Nevertheless, it does open up a range of exciting possibilities for the educational sector in the provinces.

Questions & recommendations

ICT human resource needs

According to UEM Vice-Rector Venancio Massingue, human resource needs are the biggest problem in the country in the area of ICT. While information technology is now the basic building block of all facets of the educational system – from management, to finances, to teaching, learning and research – there are not enough trained personnel in Mozambique. Massingue recommends setting up training centres for long- and short-term courses, starting first at national level and moving on to regional centres once it is possible to identify centres of excellence.[21]

The possibility of resource sharing of ICT professionals in

Mozambique could be considered a short-term strategy. UEM is probably the best-endowed university in the country in terms of ICT human capital. Most of the Mozambican librarians with degrees are at UEM; CIUEM has a versatile staff capable of handling everything from laying cable to building a home page. This is not to say that UEM has sufficient staff to handle all of its ICT needs, but its position is enviable. For example:

- UEM might serve as a resource for the Catholic University. It might be feasible for the Catholic University to send a staff member to CIUEM for a short-term attachment or internship.

- Most Mozambican lecturers teach in more than one place; they might be considered as shared resources. Could ICT personnel also be shared? For example, in Beira neither the Catholic University nor the Pedagogical University has sufficient personnel to manage its IT system. Might it be feasible to think about an agreement between the two to hire one trained IT professional to be shared between them?

Integrating ICT into the curriculum

Mozambique's universities are no different from universities elsewhere on the continent; they are only now beginning to integrate ICT into teaching and learning. There are pockets of experimentation – the Centre for Academic Development (formerly STADEP), the Faculties of Medicine and Agronomy at UEM and the new Faculty of Medicine at UCM. Could more be done, particularly on a national basis? Is this an area for more donor assistance?

The UP campus in Nampula strengthens its teaching capacity by periodically bringing in lecturers from Maputo to teach special modules. With better internet capability coming to Nampula, the impact of a physical presence could be intensified by virtual contact between visits. What about a

81

small pilot project, working with UP staff on both campuses who are already enthusiastic e-mail users?

Libraries & resource sharing

UEM has been considering the construction of a central library for many years. As stated above, one of the key recommendations in the *Strategic Plan* relates to the need for a central library. We very much hope that the entire university system will be taken into consideration as plans for the central library move forward, including the Historical Archive, the Natural History Museum and the Numismatics Museum. This is the moment to think about and plan for:

- selecting appropriate LIS packages and standardizing database architecture across the system;

- creating a common, rational appropriations policy for both books and journals. Multiple subscriptions or purchases of some materials may be necessary, for example, but duplication should be avoided unless warranted. Some materials, particularly journals and CD-ROM databases, could be made available online. An inter-library loan system could also be organized for hard copy;

- determining which materials should be placed in the central library and which materials are more appropriate to the departmental libraries;

- training and human resource requirements for the central library and each of the departmental libraries;

- even if a central library is not feasible for the moment, the UEM library system should establish a common LIS, standards, accessions policies and networked access to digital materials (on CD-ROM and the internet);

- whether the UEM central library could serve as a national reference and research library for Mozambique's higher education system. No single library anywhere in Mozambique has sufficient funding for acquisitions. Would a national higher education library consortium make sense for Mozambique?

Notes

1 See the Mozambican national profile on the *African Internet Connectivity* home page, maintained by Mike Jensen: http://www2.sn.apc.org/africa/countdet.CFM?countriesISO_Code=MZ for more information.

2 For more detailed information on EMUNet, go to http://www.uem.mz/ictproj/.

3 UEM also hopes to put six computers in each of the student dormitories and create a large networked computer room that will be available to students at all hours. Students would be able to use the computers for e-mail, internet searches, word processing, etc. A request has been made to the World Bank to make 200 reconditioned Pentium PCs available for this purpose.

4 The general site is at http://www.uem.mz/plano/index.htm. The Portuguese-language guide to the internet is found at http://www.uem.mz/pesqbibl.htm.

5 Telecentres are meant to bridge the 'digital divide' by assisting communities to communicate and access information, using technology. In Mozambique each of the two telecentres has received a public telephone; a computer with CD-ROM and software for office applications and desktop publishing; internet access; an AM/FM radio; a TV and video recorder; a photocopy machine; and a small library.

6 Go to http://www.infopol.gov.mz for more information on the development of the national ICT policy.

7 A grant from the Ford Foundation is supporting the purchase of computers and other equipment, library accessions, fitting out a new computer lab and other costs.

8 The Faculty of Medicine also expects external funding of about US$100,000 to equip the library with multimedia CD-ROMs.

9 Following the workshop, Vice-Rector Venancio Massingue proposed setting up a university-wide committee on ICT for teaching and learning. CIUEM would be responsible for the technical end, CAD for pedagogical

issues and DDS for library services.

10 Creating a university-wide library on the main campus and connecting it to national and international library networks is one of the *Strategic Plan*'s recommendations.

11 CIDOC, the Centre for Information and Documentation, now offers a medium-level three-year certificate in library studies. Graduates of the CIDOC course are considered to have the equivalent of a secondary-school diploma. CIDOC is an important step forward, but the programme still lacks sufficient computer and database training. There is a good computer lab with 20 microcomputers, but ICT does not receive sufficient attention, in part because CIDOC has been unable to identify appropriate teachers.

12 Along with everyone else, UEM's trained librarians moonlight, in this case at CIDOC, and they carry out consultancies. Even if these activities do not occur during working hours, it leaves them with less time to devote to professional tasks and research directly related to UEM.

13 CDS/ISIS is a free bibliographic software package developed by UNESCO.

14 The Historical Archive of Mozambique is already automating. As part of its participation in Projecto Memória de África, funded by the Portuguese government, the Archive received DocBase, simple-to-use and inexpensive library software developed in Portugal and based on WINISIS.

15 Of all of Mozambique's internet service providers, Teledata has had the most impact on the provinces because it has established servers in many parts of the country. Teledata subscribers in the provinces dial a local number and are then routed to the Teledata system in Maputo.

16 For information on ISRI, go to the ISRI home page:
http://www.isri.imoz.com

17 USAID is now planning to install better connectivity in Beira, Nampula and other provincial cities. This is discussed in more detail below.

18 Winnebago is widely used in US public libraries and school systems. It does not appear to have a wide international presence, however, and certainly not in Africa, which will make support and troubleshooting problematic.

19 For more information about ISPU, go to http://www.ispu.ac.mz.

20 Go to http://www.ispu.ac.mz/pesqubibl.htm.

21 UEM is beginning to move in this direction. Cisco Systems selected UEM as a regional training site for southern Africa. In addition, the CIUEM strategic plan envisages establishing an ICT institute, which would offer a two- or three-year course for mid-level technicians.

7 Finance & Governance

As stated earlier, the greatest difference between the governmental and non-governmental HEIs is the way they are
governed and financed. While the former rely almost entirely
on government and donor funding, the latter depend on
students' fees, donor support (UCM) and venture capital (ISPU,
ISCTEM and ISUTC).

Financing the governmental institutions

In 1999, the government allocated about 15 per cent of its
total expenditure to the education sector. Twenty-four per cent
of this amount went to the three governmental HEIs (UEM, UP
and ISRI). UEM took the lion's share (20 per cent), while UP
and ISRI accounted for about 3 per cent and 1 per cent
respectively (Table 21).

Table 21: HEIs' share of government education expenditure, 1999 (%)

Institution	Originally budgeted			Estimated actual		
	Recurrent	Investment	Total	Recurrent	Investment	Total
Min. Ed.	83	54	74	83	63	76
UEM	13	45	23	13	34	20
UP	3	1	2	3	4	3
ISRI	1	0	1	1	0	1
Total	100	100	100	100	100	100

Source: *Strategic Plan of Higher Education* (2000).

Current plans for the financing of education in 2000–04
indicate that in 2000 government planned to reduce the HEIs'
share of the total education budget to 14.2 per cent, down
from 24 per cent in 1999. Beyond 2000, however, it planned

to raise the share of the education budget allocated to HEIs, rising from 22.8 per cent in 2001 to 25 per cent for the next two years, and then dropping slightly to 24 per cent in 2004. In that period, the proportion of total public resources allocated to UEM, UP and ISRI would remain nearly constant, at about 20, 3, and 2.5 per cent respectively

The government plans to increase its allocation for capital investment in institutions of higher education, except for UP in 2002 and ISRI in 2004. Yet, in the case of UEM the projected allocation would cover less than half of the budget that the institution has included in its *Strategic Plan*. UEM has planned for a total of about US$123.3 million in capital investment for the 2002/2003 period, while government intends to allocate only US$50.1 million in that period.

In point of fact, UEM is heavily dependent on donor funding, which accounts for between 50 and 60 per cent of its total budget. Donors provide some 15 per cent of the ISRI budget. The Pedagogical University alone depends solely on government funding. Tuition fees constitute only a token 1 per cent of funds at UEM and 0.2 per cent at ISRI. Among the three public HEIs, only UEM has initiated income generation to augment funding from the government and donors, but the amounts realized are not significant. As a proportion of the total revenues, income generation by UEM in 1997, 1998 and 1999 was estimated at 2.7, 1.8 and 3.1 per cent respectively. In its *Strategic Plan* UEM aims to raise the ratio, but does not set any specific targets. More purposeful and rigorous efforts will therefore be needed before income generation becomes a major source of income in the public HEIs.

Financing the non-governmental HEIs

Although we do not have accurate and detailed financial information about the non-governmental institutions, a number of generalizations are possible. In the first place, tuition fees are a major source of financing. The for-profit HEIs depend entirely on fees to pay the interest on the capital raised to begin operations. The government's *Strategic Plan of Higher Education* reports that ISPU collected US$243,000 in tuition fees in 1996. That level nearly tripled the following year (US$662,000), and thereafter doubled in 1998 (US$1,224,000). ISCTEM collected US$35,730 in 1997, rising to US$75,195 in 1998 and US$139,550 in 1999.

The three non-governmental for-profit HEIs – ISTCEM, ISPU and ISUTC – maintain ties with Portuguese HEIs, which have provided financial assistance and academic cooperation, sending out teaching staff on short-term missions. The dentistry course at ISCTEM is supported, for example, by the Higher Institute of Health Sciences South, while the degree in computer science is supported by the Faculty of Science and Technology of the New University of Lisbon. Five companies with special interest in communications and transport, including Fernave of Lisbon and the Ports and Railways Company of Mozambique, finance ISUTC. ISPU, through an agreement with the Higher School of Education at Santarém (ESES) in Portugal, has received support in computerizing its libraries, the administration and the academic registry. ISPU support staff are currently undergoing training at ESES to maintain the systems.

The Italian Bishops' Conference provided funds to restore buildings and establish the courses in economics, law and education at UCM. The Portuguese Catholic Church raised over US$450,000 for the new university. This money acts as security for short-term loans that the university is now taking out to establish a faculty of medicine. Tuition fees are, however, basic to the financing of the institution and to its entire philosophy. The Rector of the Catholic University believes that students should understand that their education costs money and that they should participate actively in paying for it. He estimates that 30 per cent succeed in obtaining scholarships from their local parishes, but he is currently organizing a student loan scheme with three banks in the city of Beira to help students who lack scholarships or their own finances.

The leadership of UCM is also concerned that the institution should be self-sustaining in the long term and is reluctant to embark on projects that depend too heavily on donor support.

Unit costs

The Mozambican government has not yet developed criteria for measuring the unit costs of its institutions of higher education. The authors of the *Strategic Plan of Higher Education* calculated the average annual expenditure per student and noted that this varied considerably between the three institutions. In terms of recurrent expenditures, the unit costs range from a low of US$909 for UP to a high of US$4,677 for ISRI.

The unit costs shown in Table 22 represent estimates of the costs per student per year. To calculate unit costs per graduate, it would be necessary to multiply these figures by

Table 22: Unit costs at selected HEIs, 1999 (average per student expenditures, US$)

Category of per student expenditure	UEM	UP	ISRI, 1997–9 (average)	UCM	ISPU
Recurrent expenditure	1,778	909	4,677	1,210	1,251
Total expenditure	4,960	n.a.	6,058	n.a.	1,801
Student numbers	6,772	1,564	201	605	680

Source: *Strategic Plan of Higher Education* (2000).

the average length of study before graduation, which is considerably in excess of five years (the minimum length of study for the *licenciatura* degree), given the high rates of repetition and dropout. In 1998, only 312 students graduated from UEM, compared with a total number of 6,772. If the total expenditure of UEM (including non-recurrent development expenditure) were divided by the number of graduates rather than by the number of students, this would give the astronomical figure of over US$100,000 per graduate.

However the calculation is made, UEM and ISRI are expensive institutions in terms of their capacity to educate students when compared with the Pedagogical University and the non-governmental institutions. However, these calculations do not take into account the fact that only ISRI and UEM undertake research and that the UEM budget includes large amounts for students' scholarships and welfare. Not only does UEM charge symbolic fees; it actually pays itself for large numbers of students to study.

The issue of financial assistance to students is, as already suggested, absolutely critical to issues of equity of access to higher education. Although the fees in public HEIs are very low, students face considerable private costs, in the form of living expenses and expenditure on books and other essentials. There is very little financial assistance for students from low-income families. Only about 10 per cent of students in governmental HEIs receive scholarships and/or live in subsidized accommodation and receive assistance to purchase books.

In general, although some scholarships have been made available for private HEIs, students at these institutions pay substantial tuition fees, ranging from US$100 to US$250 per month, in addition to financing their own living costs and books. The number of scholarships or bursaries is very limited, and there is no system of student loans as yet. Fewer than 1,000 scholarships (979) were awarded in 1999 for a total of 11,619 students in all HEIs and 9,021 in governmental HEIs.

Scholarships at UEM are awarded mainly on academic merit, rather than financial need, although some donors have earmarked scholarships for women in an attempt to redress the imbalance between the sexes. A full scholarship provides assistance with fees, subsidized accommodation and books, but students may receive partial scholarships, which do not include accommodation, and/or may include reduced fees. The value of a full scholarship was MT250,000 (about US$18) a month until November 1998, when it was increased to MT353,886 (about US$25 a month, the minimum salary at that time). Since April 1999, the value of a full scholarship has been linked to the minimum salary.

Table 23: Distribution of scholarships by sex

1995		2000	
M	654	M	738
F	108	F	110
Total	762	Total	848

Source: UEM *Annual Report, 1995/6, 2000/1.*

Table 24: Distribution of scholarships by region

Region	Number of scholarships
South (Maputo, Gaza, Inhambane)	250
Centre (Sofala, Manica, Tete, Zambezia)	476
North (Nampula, Cape Delgado, Niassa)	122
Total	848

Source: Social Services Directorate, UEM.

The Social Services Directorate (DSS) at UEM provides assistance for students in the form of subsidized accommodation and meals. In 1999 the university budget allocated the DSS a total of US$23,814 for food and US$11,000 for recurrent expenses. The DSS runs six student hostels, with a total capacity of 885 places. Most of these are reserved for scholarship holders. As already stated, the system of scholarships and student welfare in general represents a considerable percentage of the university's budget.

As Tables 23 and 24 suggest, available data on scholarships are both fragmented and dispersed. For instance, whereas the Annual Report of UEM for 1995/6 makes a distinction between male and female students who hold different types of scholarships (full scholarship, partial scholarship, exemption from tuition fees and so on), the data made available by DSS for 2,000 disaggregated scholarship holders by sex and by geographic region (south, centre and north). Based on the limited information available we were able to sketch the following picture of scholarships within UEM. By and large, scholarship holders are predominantly male (86 per cent in 1995 against 87 per cent in 2000). In regional terms, available data show that the overwhelming majority (70.6 per cent) of students who held a scholarship came from the central (Sofala, Manica, Tete and Zambezia) and northern region (Nampula, Cape Delgado and Niassa) of the country. The remaining 29.5 per cent scholarship holders came from the southern region (Maputo, Gaza and Inhambane).

The non-governmental HEIs do not run their own scholarship schemes. UCM is adamant that the provision of scholarships should not be a function of the universities themselves but of specific institutions set up for that purpose. We have already referred to the Nisomé scholarship programme in the Province of Nampula and would take this opportunity to stress once again that this model might be expanded and extended to other provinces. UCM is currently in the process of negotiating a student loan scheme with the banks of Beira for which the university plans to provide the collateral.

Governance & management

The role of government

Up to the early 1990s the Ministry of Education supervised the higher education subsystem. In 1993 the Higher Education Law was enacted, establishing the autonomy of existing HEIs and setting up a mechanism for approvals of new HEIs, including, for the first time, private institutions. It also set up an advisory body, the National Council for Higher Education (CNES), comprising the rectors of all governmental and non-governmental HEIs, to advise the Council of Ministers on higher education. Responsibility for financing public HEIs lies with the Ministry of Planning and Finance. Separate negotiations for each governmental HEI take place between the senior managers of the HEI (the Rector and other key staff) and the Ministry.

The precise degree of autonomy of the governmental HEIs has often been a matter of dispute. In the case of UEM, financial autonomy was augmented in 1999 with the signing of a contract between the government and the university. Under this contract UEM receives funding quarterly, in advance, rather than monthly, as is the case in other public HEIs, and has greater freedom than before to allocate these funds. In return, the contract specifies the responsibilities and accountability of the university.

By far the most important innovation in government policy vis-à-vis higher education was the creation of a new ministry. In the wake of the mushrooming growth of HEIs and in view of the apparent inability of the CNES to address the new challenges, the government established the Ministry of Higher Education, Science and Technology (MESCT) in January 2000, with the objective of developing legal and regulatory mechanisms to ensure the effective implementation of national policies for higher education and research. While respecting the institutional autonomy of individual HEIs, the government is committed to:

- reviewing existing higher education laws, statutes and regulations in the light of changing circumstances;
- defining norms for the establishment of HEIs and courses;
- defining an accreditation system for higher education;
- developing a national policy on science and technology, including scientific research;
- ensuring that statutes and regulations are consistent with national policies on institutional autonomy and account-ability, financing and quality assurance;
- obliging all HEIs to submit regular strategic plans and reports to the MESCT;
- encouraging coordination between HEIs and research institutes;
- reviewing salaries to ensure that relevant vocational abilities are considered along with academic qualifications;
- defining policy and legislation for higher education workers, to ensure stability of employment and market competitive-ness;
- adopting a policy of fiscal benefits, with exemption or reduction of fiscal obligations to private HEIs, aimed at promoting their expansion.

The government is also committed to promoting and facilitating regional integration and multilateral and inter-national cooperation within the sphere of higher education. In this regard, the MESCT is currently promoting the exchange of academic and scientific programmes at both regional and

93

international levels. It has also started acting as the facilitator between HEIs and donors, investors and companies in order to establish partnerships.

Although non-governmental HEIs are gradually contributing to meeting the growing demand for higher education, government HEIs, especially public universities, are expected to take the lead through the combination of teaching and research tasks. Research carried out by public HEIs is perceived as critical to the production of fundamental and applied knowledge. The government is keen to see this role further expanded and consolidated through the opening of postgraduate studies in public HEIs.

Led by a former vice-rector of the UEM, the new Ministry initiated its activities with a number of consultative meetings, which were called to discuss policy and research for higher education. President Joaquim Chissano, in a clear sign of presidential support for the new ministry and its mission, opened the first meeting, held in July 2000. The *Strategic Plan of Higher Education* formed the basis for discussions that brought together not only the major actors in all the HEIs in the country but also officials from each province.

Although the meeting did not result in firm decisions, it did confirm the enormous political importance of higher education. Each province demanded its own HEI, ostensibly to meet the increasing demand from secondary-school leavers. It became increasingly clear that provincial leaders see institutions of higher education as important symbols of prestige and engines of development. The second meeting was a national seminar on research policy, held in October 2000. It allowed the new Ministry to develop a comprehensive picture of the current stage of technological development and knowledge production in Mozambique. It also laid a solid foundation for the establishment in Mozambique of a database on scientific and technological activity, to support science and technology policy planning and implementation. Finally, the meeting suggested a number of methodologies for science and technology policy formulation, including the setting of short- and medium-term priorities.

A third series of round-table meetings was held during February and March 2001 in Beira, Pemba and Maputo. The meetings were jointly organized by the MESCT, the Centre for Higher Education Policy Studies (CHEPS) of the University of Twente, and Professor Dick Richardson of New York University, with the financial support of the Royal Netherlands Embassy in Maputo, the Ford Foundation and the World Bank. The purpose of these meetings was to initiate a national debate on a diversified and flexible system of higher education in Mozambique that would allow more equitable access and higher quality, together with greater relevance and higher efficiency. The Mozambican participants, who included academics, government officials, educators, the business community and representatives of civil society, were drawn from every province of the country.

The round tables focused on how to structure a new higher education system that would address the following objectives of the *Strategic Plan*:

- provision of higher education based on provincial or regional needs and preferences for specialized human resources;
- diversification and decentralization of programmes, courses and degree structure in terms of level, duration, academic and professional focus;
- decentralization of the process of policy formulation.

In the initial phase of its development, the system would rely on a central coordinating unit that would work to decentralize some operational aspects to local levels. Decisions about the number of students to be admitted in each programme would be the responsibility of each HEI based on its capacities, market opportunities and national needs. The initiative to open new programmes falling outside its mandate would be the responsibility of each HEI, but the final decision would be the responsibility of the central coordinating unit at the higher education subsystem level. The government will set up financial and legal mechanisms to influence coordination between institutions and approve the introduction of priority courses/programmes and the number of students.

The Minister hopes that this and other series of meetings will result in the formation of policy with the active cooperation of all the major stakeholders.

Governance & management of public institutions

The organizational structures and functions of public HEIs are all very similar. The University Council (UC) is the top decision-making body in public HEIs and is chaired by the Rector. At UEM, the UC is composed of:

- the Rector, as chair;
- the Vice-Rector for Resources and Administration (*ex-officio*);
- the Vice-Rector for Academic Affairs (*ex-officio*);
- three representatives of deans of faculties, elected by the Council of Directors/Deans;
- four representatives of assistant, associate and full professors, elected by all professors;
- three representatives of junior and senior lecturers, elected by the lecturers;
- two student representatives;
- one representative of centres, elected by the directors of centres;
- two representatives of non-academic trade unions;
- five members selected from civil society;
- three members appointed by the government;
- the Director of the Museum of Natural History;

- the Director of the national Historical Archive.

The Rector is the academic and administrative leader of the university and is accountable to the UC, with the support of the Academic Council (AC), the Vice-Rector for Resources and Administration and the Vice-Rector for Academic Affairs.

The UC normally meets twice a year and extraordinarily whenever the Rector deems it necessary. It has the overall responsibility for recommending to the President of the Republic names for the Rector's and the Vice-Rectors' posts; instituting or rationalizing university courses; approving annual academic and financial plans as well as long-term plans; examining the annual accounts; recommending adjustments to UEM's statutes after consultation with the AC; approving regulations and policies resulting from the statutes; deciding on fundamental matters regarding the university's patrimony; appointing leaders for specific initiatives; and appointing sub-commissions of the UC.

The AC deals with all academic affairs (research, curriculum development, postgraduate training plans, academic promotions, etc). However, the terms of reference of this body need to be clarified and revised, and the division of responsibilities between the AC and the faculties is one of the major outstanding issues in the administration of public HEIs.

The AC is chaired by the Rector and includes the two Vice-Rectors. It also includes representatives of different areas of expertise. Like the UC, the AC meets twice a year and extraordinarily whenever the Rector deems it necessary. It is responsible for academic policy, the regulation and quality of courses, teaching and examinations. The Council has the power and duty to prepare annual academic plans; encourage and promote research; stimulate inter-faculty developments; determine policy and regulate the admission of students; recommend academic plans and budgets; analyse postgraduate

97

plans (doctoral); formulate and recommend reorganization of academic departments and faculties; make academic regulations; comment on and make recommendations to the UC on proposed changes to UEM statutes; appoint committees and delegate functions to other committees or individuals; and carry out any other function authorized by the UC

UEM has centres that are linked to the faculties. Examples of these centres are the Centre of Habitat Studies and Development, which is linked to the Faculty of Architecture and Physical Planning; the Centre of Engineering Studies linked to the Faculty of Engineering; the Centre of Studies of Population and the Land Studies Unit, linked to the Faculty of Arts. Enjoying increasing degrees of financial autonomy, the centres are perhaps the most dynamic nodes of activity within the university.

Following the massive exodus of Portuguese personnel in 1975, UEM, as already noted, relied on expatriate staff from different countries, especially from the former Soviet Union and East Germany. With very few Mozambican staff members in key positions in the administration and management of the university, there was a need to create a central management structure capable of regulating and inspecting both the academic and administrative activities. On the other hand, due to the shortage of infrastructure and adequate support systems in the country, the government decided that UEM should take on responsibility for a number of services that under normal conditions would not be part of a university system, such as transport, petrol supplies, accommodation and catering services.

The survival management approach that was adopted after independence was followed by a period of approximately ten years of relative stability, with *The Present and Perspectives* strategic plan as a crucial instrument. During this period centralized management was still in place, although some units had started to exercise some autonomy.

The prevailing management model was characterized by:

- excessive centralization of resources and decision-making processes;
- extremely centralized budget and finance management;
- difficulty in retaining technically qualified and professionally capable personnel.

For instance, over 70 per cent of the state budget allocated for running costs was managed at the central level, with less than 30 per cent allocated to faculties.

An in-depth analysis of the current situation, within the framework of the 1999 strategic planning exercise and the ongoing Netherlands-funded Reform of University Management and Administration project (RUMA) project, concluded that various UEM academic units had increased the number and qualifications of their staff to a level that made them able to face the challenges and responsibilities of decentralized administration and management. Despite progress towards decentralization, however, a number of problems persisted, some of which had been identified in previous studies, including in 1992 the Commonwealth Secretariat *Review of Governance, Planning and Management* funded by the Special Commonwealth Fund for Mozambique and the Ford Foundation. The most salient problems identified include:

- the absence of a conceptual model for administration and institutional management;
- lack of integration of administration and management into one system;
- unclear administrative legislation;
- excessive centralization of decision-making, with the Rector's office and the central directorates controlling the units;
- accumulation of financial and material resources at the

central level, inhibiting academic units' abilities to act
effectively;

- inadequate use of information and communication technology as a tool for increased efficiency in administrative and
financial management;
- excessive number of administrative and support staff with
education and training levels below the minimum requirements for adequate performance;
- inadequate communication systems resulting in lack of
coordination between management and administration.

The RUMA project is now addressing these and other
persisting challenges. Funded by the Netherlands Organization
for Cooperation in Higher Education, RUMA aims to support
UEM in reforming its management and administration
structures in order to achieve a transparent, effective and
efficient organization and create the management capacity to
sustain the system. In addition to the UEM, other organizations participating in this project are CHEPS of the University
of Twente and the Centre for International Cooperation (CIS)
of the Free University of Amsterdam. A project management
team comprising representatives of UEM and CHEPS and a
UEM Task Force on management and administrative reform
have been set up. Consultative meetings between the project
management and the UEM community take place on a regular
basis.

Governance & management in private institutions

ISPU, ISUTC and ISCTEM have similar organizational structures.
The Rector is responsible for decision-making, supported by
the Scientific Council for Academic Affairs, which is similar to
the Academic Council in the governmental institutions. ISPU
has two schools, one for Management and Technology with
nine courses, and another for Law and Social Sciences with
seven courses. Two directors manage these schools.

100

UCM depends on the Catholic Education Congregation and the Episcopal Conference of Mozambique. The governance of UCM is the responsibility of the Chancellor, the Rector and one or more Vice-Rectors. The Chancellor is the Archbishop of Beira, who is the spiritual leader, promoting religion within the university community. The Rector, who has the same mandate as the rectors of the governmental institutions, is nominated by the Mozambican Episcopal Conference. The Rector is accountable to the University Council, which is led by the Chancellor, and is supported by the Rectorate Council and the Financial Management Council. The Rectorate Council is led by the Rector, and includes the Vice-Rectors, the directors of regional centres and the general secretary of the university. It assists the Rector in every issue related to the university and promulgates university regulations. The Financial Management Council, over which the Rector presides, includes the Vice-Rector, representatives of each regional centre, two institutional representatives designated by the Chancellor, and the General Secretary of the university. This council has an Executive Council, which takes care of the budget and running costs.

A director who represents the Rector, supported by an Administrative Committee, an executive secretariat and an Academic Council, leads the branch campuses or regional centres of UCM. The Administrative Committee, which deals with the financial management of the centre, is led by the director of the centre and is composed of the directors of the basic units, course coordinators, institutional representatives chosen by the UCM and the secretary of the centre. The director, the secretary of the centre and three other nominated governing staff members comprise the executive secretariat of the regional centre. This secretariat deals with daily management, current costs, and the execution of the budget and the accounts.

The Academic Council of the regional centre is chaired by

the director of the centre and is composed of the directors of the basic units, directors of departments, course coordinators, one lecturer for each course, presidents of the student associations, one student from each course, the director of social services and the secretary of the centre. The director, board of directors and Scientific Council lead each basic unit. The Scientific Council is composed of the president, full, associate and assistant professors. UCM also has study centres, headed by directors appointed by the Rector, for applied and pure scientific research, teaching and service delivery.

8 Conclusions & Recommendations

A dynamic field

Amazing progress has been made in higher education in post-independence Mozambique. After the initial hiatus caused by the exodus of the Portuguese, the socialist interlude, the long years of bitter civil war and then the extenuating efforts required to adjust to a market-driven economy and a democratic political order, Mozambique now possesses a higher education system that offers a wide variety of course options, undertakes first-rate research in some areas, and, although concentrated in the capital city of Maputo, is also present in four outlying provinces.

Equity of access

Regrettably all these institutions cater to a minute fraction of the Mozambican population. They are responsible for training the tiny elite that will be prominent in government, in political parties, in non-governmental organizations and in the professions, industry and commerce.

A major problem is that the majority of the students who succeed in entering governmental and non-governmental HEIs are the sons and daughters of relatively well-to-do families (in Mozambican terms). Perhaps the most dramatic finding of this report is that nearly 80 per cent of university students in Mozambique use Portuguese as their principal means of communication. HEIs thus fulfil the role of establishing, reproducing and consolidating a hereditary elite.

Within this tiny elite, some social categories are present more than others. We have shown, for example, that people from the northern and central provinces of the country have fewer chances to enter the governmental universities than those from the southern provinces, in particular from the city of Maputo. We have also shown that women have less of a chance than men to enter institutions of higher learning, especially the public ones.

103

In order to improve equity of access, we have a number of suggestions to make.

Rationalize existing scholarship arrangements & establish student loan facilities

At present UEM runs its own scholarship programme funded by donors and the government, which caters for a small number of students. There is little evidence that it has done much to correct imbalances of socio-economic class, gender and regional origin in the student population. The most successful and interesting scheme that we observed was Nisomé in the province of Nampula. We suggest that similar schemes be established in all provinces, with funding from the provinces themselves, donors (each province has quite specific donors) and central government. Each provincial fund would be run by a non-governmental board, overseen by the Ministry of Higher Education. Such a scheme would automatically address the issue of regional imbalance. Guidelines for local committees would be established to address gender and social-class inequalities.

At the moment there are no student loan schemes available in Mozambique, although the Catholic University has made overtures to banks in the city of Beira. We recommend that a simple but reliable student loan system be introduced with considerable urgency. We also recommend student fees and a national loan scheme as a subject for further study.

As these two mechanisms are brought into effect, the governmental institutions might start charging fees compatible with those of the non-governmental institutions. We understand that such a decision would probably be extremely unpopular, since it would signal yet another capitulation to market forces. But the government might prefer to provide support to its own university through the medium of student loans and scholarships rather than only through direct grants. This is evidently a contentious issue, and we make the suggestion in the spirit of wishing to initiate a debate.

Undertake a review of entrance examination procedures

A number of people to whom we talked felt that the entrance exams to all institutions of higher education favour students who have retentive memories and who have had the privilege of attending good governmental and non-governmental schools. We suggest that alternative means of evaluation be considered that would pay due attention to intellectual aptitude and personal predisposition toward certain programmes.

Diversify the existing higher education subsystem

The emergence of new and non-traditional HEIs closer to the local communities should be encouraged. These institutions should be able to respond more rapidly and flexibly to the demands and expectations of the public and private sectors and non-governmental organizations for a trained workforce, while addressing both regional and socio-economic imbalances in the country.

Expanding access to higher education can be achieved through evening and residential courses for those from outlying areas, as well as distance and open learning courses. We therefore strongly recommend that a study on distance higher education be carried out very shortly.

Teaching staff

The government, donors and non-governmental HEIs have taken important steps to train highly qualified teaching staff. The dependence of most non-governmental HEIs on teachers 'drained' from the governmental institutions has the effect of reducing the research potential of the governmental institutions, while enhancing teaching quality in the non-governmental institutions.

National Science Research Fund

To safeguard and promote research and to guarantee dedication to teaching and research on the part of university teachers, we also suggest that the Ministry of Higher Education, Science and Technology establish a national science research fund to provide funding for research in general but also research scholarships for individual researchers. In principle, this would allow faculty members at a public university to dedicate themselves full-time to their research and students without having to moonlight. Some examples of interesting work carried out by UEM staff that need to be encouraged include publications and ongoing research by the History Department, the Centre for African Studies, the Linguistics Department, the Faculty of Agronomy, the Faculty of Medicine and the recently reopened UEM Faculty of Education, to name but a few.

Curriculum, teaching methods & relevance

We found that the governmental institutions, in particular UEM, have developed their own critique of curricula and teaching methods and are in the process of implementing changes. UEM faces the problem of reconciling its role as the country's only full-blown university with demands for immediate market relevance. Owing to their dependence on students' fees for survival, the non-governmental HEIs are obliged to offer courses that are perceived to be relevant. Even so, there are differences of approach between the denominational Catholic University and the for-profits institutions (we have no information on the Islamic University). While the for-profits are closely geared to market forces, UCM is driven also by Christian ideals of service and community development.

Universities involved in curriculum reform are encouraged to take steps to ensure student mobility and a more rational use of existing teaching and learning facilities and resources on campus. There are different ways in which student mobility can be facilitated and enhanced. These include the development and use of improved entrance examinations and selection criteria; the coordination and harmonization of

106

degree structures and the content of similar programmes between institutions of higher education; and the development and use of comparable credit unit systems across the higher education system. On the other hand, a more rational use of learning facilities and resources on campus may involve the development of inter- and multi-disciplinary courses and research programmes, starting at postgraduate level, and contracts for the use of existing teaching materials, teaching staff and physical facilities (e.g. libraries, science labs, computer labs, sports facilities, etc).

Distance learning

Upon conclusion of relevant feasibility studies, the Ministry of Higher Education, Science and Technology should appoint an installation committee for distance higher education in Mozambique. In addition to laying the foundations for a future Open University of Mozambique, such a committee should act as a focal point for all HEIs interested in open and distance learning.

Information and communication technologies

Although UEM has been well in advance of most African universities in the field of information technology, we cannot overemphasize our disappointment at its relatively slow dissemination at Mozambique's other universities. For this vast country with its poor infrastructure and dispersed faculties, a more complete utilization of the internet (including e-mail) and electronic databases is essential to the expansion of quality higher education and the development of a sophisticated research community. As far as libraries are concerned, we must also express our dismay. With the exception of a few subject-specific libraries at UEM, we found insufficient collections, much irrelevant material and no intra-institutional cooperation.

Taking into account this situation, we strongly recommend the sharing of ICT facilities (including VSAT, internet and library facilities), especially among governmental HEIs. We

107

also endorse UEM's plan to expand its library capability by building a central library open to other HEIs and the general public in Maputo.

A final word: energies

During the study we observed that the field of higher education in Mozambique could be divided into governmental and non-governmental institutions, with the former dependent on government and donor support and the latter on students' fees. Governmental institutions may be further subdivided into the one full-scale university (UEM), a teacher-training university (UP) and three specialized independent faculties – ISRI, the Police Academy and the Nautical School. The non-governmental institutions may be subdivided into denominational establishments (the Catholic University and Mussa bin Bik Islamic University) and for-profit institutions (ISPU, ISCTEM and ISUTC). Of these, only UCM can claim to be in the process of becoming a university in the traditional sense of the term.

After visiting all these institutions we were most impressed by their vitality. While all are dedicated to the training of young Mozambicans and espouse the traditional values of higher education (their mission statements are strikingly similar), each has its own specific energy. The governmental institutions thrive on a tradition of public service and an ideology of disinterested quality; the for-profit institutions derive their energy from the need to survive financially and hopefully to make money, but they also aim for social recognition and prestige. The denominational institutions derive much of their energy from religious conviction.

In conclusion, we strongly recommend that government and donors recognize these varied approaches and energies, which in combination result in a diverse and vital field of higher education in Mozambique.

Appendix 1
People We Met

Abudo, José Ibraimo. Minister of Justice and founder of Mussa bin Bik University. Met in Maputo.

Amade, Fátima. Adviser to the Minister for Higher Education, Science and Technology, Maputo

Amos, Gabriel. Dean, Faculty of Engineering, UEM, Maputo

Andrade, Osvaldo Camacho. Research Assistant, UEM, Maputo

Assale, João Alfredo Gueredate. Director, Faculty of Agriculture, UCM, Cuamba

Behrens, Inês. Housing Officer, Faculty of Agriculture, UCM, Cuamba

Born, Timothy. Infrastructure Division Chief, United States Agency for International Development

Bregueje, Mariano. Director, ISPU, Quelimane

Brito, Lídia Maria Ribeiro Arthur. Minister of Higher Education, Science and Technology, Maputo

Brito, Rui. Director, Faculty of Agronomy, UEM, Maputo

Buque, Ambrósio. Headmaster, Josina Machel Secondary School, Maputo

Carrilho, Lara. Deputy Dean, Faculty of Agronomy, UEM, Maputo

Carvalho, André Nunes de. Rector, ISUTC, Maputo

Cassy, Bhangy. Research Assistant, UEM, Maputo

Castiano, José P. UP, Maputo

Coelho, João Paulo Borges. History Lecturer, UEM, Maputo

Couto, Filipe. Rector, UCM, Beira

Culpa, Virgílio. Lecturer in Mathematics, Faculty of Science, UEM, Maputo

Diniz, Célia. Representative, African-American Institute, Maputo

Diniz, Maria João Carrilho. Headmistress, Kitabu Secondary School, Maputo

Draisma, Jan. Mathematics Lecturer, UP, Beira

Estunco, Conde. Dean of Economics and Administration, UCM, Beira

Fautino, Humberto. Faculty of Medicine, UEM, Maputo

Ferrão, Pedro. KPMG Employment Agency, Maputo

Filimone, Luzidia. Lecturer in Modern Literature, Faculty of Arts, UEM, Maputo

Francisco, Romão. Assistant Registrar, Faculty of Arts, UEM, Maputo

Garrido, Paulo Ivo. Rector, ISCTEM, Maputo

Groosjohan, Bernard. Dean, Faculty of Medicine, UCM, Beira

Guiamba, Sandra Bernardo. Research Assistant, UEM, Maputo

Gumanánze, Octávia Vieira. Librarian, ISPU, Quelimane

Issak, Aissa. Director, Directorate for Documentation Services, UEM, Maputo

Ivala, Adelino. Director, UP, Nampula

José, Patrício. Vice-Rector, ISRI, Maputo

Kouwenhoven, Wim. Chemistry Educator, Staff Development Project, UEM, Maputo

Leopoldo, Joao. Deputy Dean, Faculty of Medicine, UEM, Maputo

Mabila, Francisco. Deputy Director, CIUEM, UEM, Maputo

Machili, Carlos. Rector, UP, Maputo

Mahave, Moisés. Housing Department staff member, UEM, Maputo

Mandlate, Ernesto. Coordinator, Staff Development Programme, UEM, Maputo

Mangrasse, Lucas. Deputy Director, UP, Nampula
Martins, Emília. Head of the Housing Department, UEM, Maputo
Massinga, Pedro Jr. Chairman, Students' Association, UEM, Maputo
Massingue, Venâncio. Vice-Rector, UEM, Maputo
Mazula, Brazão. Rector, UEM, Maputo
Meque, Alexandre. Director, 25 de Setembro School, Quelimane
Moet, Joop. Lecturer, Faculty of Agriculture, UCM, Cuamba
Mondego, Celeste. Director, Delta Secondary School, Maputo
Morais, Maria Emília. Pedagogical Director, ISCTEM, Maputo
Mubai, Marlino. Students' Association representative, Faculty of Arts, UEM, Maputo
Mucavele, Firmino. Lecturer in Agrarian Economics, Faculty of Agronomy, UEM, Maputo
Muchanga, Americo. Director, CIUEM, UEM, Maputo
Parbato, Danilo. Director of Public Relations, ISCTEM, Maputo
Pedro, Lídia Titos. Research Assistant, UEM, Maputo
Pinto, Maria Alice. Secretary, Installation Committee, Faculty of Education, UEM, Maputo
Plumerel, Joelle. English Teacher, Faculty of Agriculture, UCM, Cuamba
Ponsi, Francesco. Vice-Rector, UCM, Beira
Portugal, Lina. Director, Samora Moises Machel Secondary School, Beira
Rosário, Lourenço do. Rector, ISPU, Maputo
Rothemberger, Augusto. KPMG Employment Agency, Maputo
Rougles, William P. Computer Specialist, UCM, Beira
Rulkens, Tom. Lecturer in Crop Production, Faculty of Agriculture, UCM, Cuamba
Sacate, Rute Julieta. Administrative Officer, Faculty of Arts, UEM, Maputo
Sambo, Vitorino. Head of the History Department, Faculty of Arts, UEM, Maputo
Schultheis, Michael J. Lecturer in Economics, UCM, Beira
Schwalbach, João. Dean, Faculty of Medicine, UEM, Maputo
Silva, Rosania da. Public Relations Officer, ISPU, Maputo
Silva, Teresa Cruz e. Director, Centre for African Studies, UEM, Maputo
Soares, Daniel. Director, UP, Beira
Souto, Amelia Neves de. Documentalist, Centre for African Studies, UEM, Maputo
Stephens, Jeanne. CEO, Austral Employment Agency, Maputo
Sumbana, Glória. Director, Academic Registry, ISPU, Quelimane
Taímo, Jamisse. Rector, ISRI, Maputo
Tajú, Gulamo. Deputy Dean, UFICS, UEM, Maputo
Uamba, Sozinho Israel. Assistant Registrar, UFICS, UEM, Maputo
Valcarcel, Carmen. Pedagogical Director, ISPU, Quelimane
Vengwa, Emannuel. Librarian, UCM, Beira
Vilela, Ana. Coordinator, ISPU Quelimane Branch. Met in Maputo.
Zamba, David. Assistant Registrar, Faculty of Economics, UEM, Maputo
Zeca, Alberto. CEO, International Computer Systems, Ltd and Lecturer, ISPU, Quelimane

Appendix 2
Survey Questionnaire to Students in HEIs in Mozambique

1. In which university are you currently enrolled? _____
2. What is your current undergraduate status? 1. Full-time student ❑ 2. Part-time student ❑
3. Are you in paid employment? 1. Yes ❑ 2. No ❑
4. If so, how many hours do you work per week? _____
5. If so, how much do you earn per month? _____
6. How many years of university education have you already completed successfully?
   1. Less than a year ❑ 2. Just one year ❑ 3. Two years ❑ 4. Three years ❑ 5. Four years ❑
7. How many times have you changed your major study programme since you were first admitted in higher education? 1. Never changed ❑ 2. Changed once ❑ 3. Changed twice ❑
8. If you have ever changed your major programme, what was (were) the reason(s)? _____
9. In which one of the following faculties/schools are you currently enrolled?
   1. Architecture ❑ 2. Agronomy ❑ 3. Arts ❑ 4. Economics ❑ 5. Education/Pedagogy ❑
   6. Engineering ❑ 7. International Relations ❑ 8. Law ❑ 9. Medicine ❑ 10. Natural Science ❑
   11. Social Sciences ❑ 12. Veterinary Science ❑ 13. Another ❑ Which one? _____
10. What year did you enter this faculty/school? _____
11. What is the main source of financial support for your study?
    1. My parents or relatives ❑ 2. Government scholarship ❑ 3. Private scholarship ❑
    4. Philanthropy (donor organization) ❑ 5. Loan ❑ 6. My employer ❑ 7. My own earnings ❑
    8. Other ❑ Which one(s)? _____
12. If any individual or institution helped you financially with your studies, who or which one? _____
13. If any individual or institution helped you financially with your studies, how much? _____
14. Are you responsible for contributing financially to the support of other members of your family?
    1. Yes ❑ 2. No ❑
15. If so, for whom? _____
16. If so, how much do you contribute per month? _____
17. Where do you live during the school year?
    1. With my parents or relatives ❑ 2. In a residence hall (on campus) ❑ 3. In a boarding house ❑
    4. In a shared apartment (off campus) ❑ 5. In my own house/apartment ❑
18. What were your scores on the entrance examinations on the 0–20 point scale?
    1. Biology ❑ 2. Chemistry ❑ 3. Mathematics ❑ 4. Physics ❑ 5. Portuguese ❑ 6. Geography ❑
    7. History ❑ 8. English ❑
19. In which pre-university school (11th/12th grade) did you study before entering the university?
    1. Francisco Manyanga (Maputo) ❑ 2. Josina Machel (Maputo) ❑ 3. Xai-xai (Gaza) ❑
    4. Emília Daússe (Inhambane) ❑ 5. Joaquim Mara (Manica) ❑ 6. Samora Machel (Sofala) ❑
    7. 1° de Maio (Nampula) ❑ 8. E.S. de Tete (Tete) ❑ 9. 25 de Setembro (Zambezia) ❑
    10. F. Samuel Kankhomba (Niassa) ❑ 11. E. S. de Pemba (Cape Delgado) ❑
    12. Instituto Industrial (Maputo) ❑ 13. Instituto Comercial (Maputo) ❑ 14. Other – Which one? ❑
20. What is your current undergraduate Grade Point Average (GPA) on the 0-20 points scale?
    1. Mostly **19-20** points ❑ 2. Mostly **17-18** points ❑ 3. Mostly **14-16** point ❑
    4. Mostly **11-13** points ❑ 5. Mostly **9-10** points ❑
21. Have you ever dropped out of your major study programme since you were admitted to higher education?
    1. Once ❑ 2. Twice ❑ 3. Never ❑
22. If so, which discipline(s) have you failed? _____
23. Listed below is a number of factors related to your satisfaction with the education that you get in your school/faculty. Based on your experience, tell us how satisfied you feel on each of these factors. Circle **1** if you are **Very satisfied**; Circle **2** if you are **Satisfied**; Circle **3** if you are **Undecided**; Circle **4** if you are **Dissatisfied**; Circle **5** if you are **Very dissatisfied**.

A. Courses and Curriculum	1	2	3	4	5
B. Quality of instruction	1	2	3	4	5
C. Knowledge, teaching skills and personal qualities of instructors	1	2	3	4	5
D. Books and learning conditions in the library	1	2	3	4	5
E. Amount and quality of attention and feedback from instructors	1	2	3	4	5
F. Methods and criteria of student evaluation	1	2	3	4	5

G. Computational facilities available	1	2	3	4	5
H. My intellectual development	1	2	3	4	5
I. The development of my study skills and work habits	1	2	3	4	5
J. Social life within the school/university	1	2	3	4	5
K. Sports and recreational	1	2	3	4	5
L. The prestige of my faculty/school	1	2	3	4	5
M. Transport and communication facilities	1	2	3	4	5
N. Food and residence services	1	2	3	4	5

Comments:

24. Listed below are some statements related to particular instances of your educational experience in your school. Please indicate whether or not these statements correspond to the way in which you feel about your last year's (or last semester's) experience at school by selecting 1 for **"Was my experience"** or 2 for **"Was not my experience"**.

A. Courses were harder than I expected	1	2
D. I learned a lot	1	2
B. Courses were interesting	1	2
E. I met a lot of people with new ideas	1	2
C. I performed well academically	1	2

Comments:

25. Listed below is a set of decisions that could help improve the functioning of the library in your school/faculty. Please, **circle 1** the two decisions that you consider a **first priority**; **circle 2** the two decisions that you consider a **second** priority; **circle 3** the two decisions that you consider the **third priority**; **circle 4** the two decisions that you consider the **fourth priority**.

A. To increase the number of books and journals in the library	1	2	3	4
B. To increase the number of copies for each title in the library	1	2	3	4
C. To increase the number of titles in Portuguese language	1	2	3	4
D. To increase the number of titles in English	1	2	3	4
E. To increase the number of titles in French	1	2	3	4
F. To diversify the authors of books in the library	1	2	3	4
G. To increase the number of journals in my discipline or specialization	1	2	3	4
H. To increase the number of service hours of the library	1	2	3	4
I. To increase the space and number of seats in the library	1	2	3	4
J. To change the procedures of access to the books and other study materials	1	2	3	4
K. To make photocopying facilities available to the students at an affordable price	1	2	3	4
L. To introduce a system of managing information that will allow everyone to rapidly locate the existing books in the library	1	2	3	4
M. To introduce a more rigorous and effective system for registering and monitoring the books that have been borrowed	1	2	3	4
N. To improve the level of academic and professional training of the staff	1	2	3	4
O. To involve students in the management of the library	1	2	3	4

26. What is the highest level of primary, secondary, technical, or post-secondary education attained by your father?
27. What is the highest level of primary, secondary, technical, or post-secondary education attained by your mother?
28. Please provide an overall estimate of your household monthly income.
29. What is your father's occupation? _____
30. What is your mother's occupation? _____
31. Where did your parents or close relatives live for the last five years? _____
32. If you are a part-time student, what is your occupation? _____
33. Which language did you learn to speak first?
    1. African-Bantu ❑ 2. Portuguese ❑ 3. Other ❑ Which one? _____
34. How often do you use your mother/parental tongue to communicate with your parents and other relatives at home? 1. Always ❑ 2. Very often ❑ 3. Occasionally ❑ 4. Never ❑
35. How often do you use Portuguese to communicate with your parents and other relatives at home?
    1. Always ❑ 2. Very often ❑ 3. Occasionally ❑ 4. Never ❑

36. How often do you use English as a medium of communication in the classroom?
   1. Always ❑   2. Very often ❑   3. Occasionally ❑   4. Never ❑
37. Do you use e-mail?
   1. Yes ❑   2. No ❑
38. Where do you send and receive e-mail messages?
   1. Computer laboratory/centre ❑   2. Library ❑   3. Home ❑   4. Other ❑   Please specify _____
40. How often do you use e-mail?   1. Every day ❑   2. At least once a week ❑   3. Occasionally ❑
41. With whom do you communicate using e-mail? 1. Friends ❑   2. Lecturers ❑   3. Friends and family ❑
42. Do you use Internet for online searching? 1. Yes ❑   2. No ❑
43. If so, for what purpose? (Please describe) _____
44. Are students required to use computers in your faculty/school? 1. Yes ❑   2. No ❑   3. Don't know ❑
45. Were you familiar with computers and computer technology before entering the university?
   1. Very familiar ❑   2. Just enough ❑   3. A little ❑   4. Not at all ❑
46. Did you receive any training in computer technology in your faculty/school? 1. Yes ❑   2. No ❑
47. What do you usually do with computers? 1. Type papers ❑   2. Crunch data ❑   3. Play games ❑
   4. Other activities ❑   Which ones? _____
48. Listed below are some statements related to the functioning of the laboratories in your university.
   Please circle 1 if you **fully agree**; circle 2 if you **agree**; circle 3 if you are **undecided**; circle 4 if you **disagree**; circle 5 if you **disagree completely**.
   A. The size of the laboratories matches The number of students in my class   1 2 3 4 5
   B. Laboratories are well equipped and maintained
   C. We never run short of reagents and other consumables in the labs   1 2 3 4 5
   D. Lab staff is technically well prepared and professionally competent   1 2 3 4 5
   E. Lab staff is always available and ready to help me   1 2 3 4 5
   F. So far my laboratory classes have been well prepared and implemented   1 2 3 4 5
   G. My scientific abilities and interest for science have increased a lot since I entered
      the university   1 2 3 4 5
49. If you are a part-time student, what year did you start working? _____
50. How would describe your race/color?
   1. Black ❑   2. White (Caucasian) ❑   3 Asian ❑   4. Mixed ❑   5. Other ❑   Which one? _____
51. What year were you born? _____
52. What is your sex? 1. Female ❑   2. Male ❑
53. How many brothers and sisters did you have? Please count those born alive, but no longer living, as well as those alive now. Also include stepbrothers and stepsisters and children adopted by your parents. _____
54. What is your marital status? 1. Single ❑   2. Married ❑   3. Widowed ❑   4. Divorced ❑   5. Separated ❑
55. If you were asked to use one of the following names for your social class, which would you say you belong in?   1. Lower class ❑   2. Working class ❑   3. Middle class ❑   4. Upper class ❑   5. Don't know
56. What is your religious affiliation/preference?
   1. Animist ❑   2. Catholic ❑   3. Hindu ❑   4. Muslim ❑   5. Protestant ❑   6. None ❑   7. Other ❑
   Which one? _____
57. What is your nationality?   1. Mozambican citizen ❑   2. Foreign citizen ❑
58. In which province were you born?
   1. Maputo ❑   2. Maputo City ❑   3. Gaza ❑   4. Inhambane ❑   5. Manica ❑   6. Sofala ❑
   7. Zambezia ❑   8. Tete ❑   9. Cape Delgado ❑   10. Niassa ❑   11. Another place – Which one?
59. How would you describe your birthplace? 1. Urban ❑   2. Semi-rural ❑   3. Rural ❑
60. What would you like to do after graduation?
   1. Work for a private company ❑   2. Work for a government/parastatal organization ❑
   3. Work for an international organization ❑   4. Work for a non-governmental organization (NGO) ❑
   5. Be self-employed ❑   6. Go to graduate school ❑   7. Don't know/undecided
61. In the space below please write any comments that you may wish to make:
   _____
   _____

113

References

Commonwealth Secretariat. *Review of Governance, Planning and Management.* London: The Commonwealth Secretariat and the Ford Foundation, 1992.

Eduardo Mondlane University. 1991. *The Present and Perspectives for the Future* Vols. 1 and 2. [Published in Portuguese as *Presente e perspectivas*]. Maputo: UEM.

——. 1992. *Annual Report 1991–1992.* Maputo: UEM.

——. 1993. *Annual Report 1992–1993.* Maputo: UEM.

——. 1994. *Annual Report 1993–1994.* Maputo: UEM.

——. 1995. *Annual Report 1994–1995.* Maputo: UEM.

——. 1996. *Annual Report 1995–1996.* Maputo: UEM.

——. 1997. *Annual Report 1996–1997.* Maputo: UEM.

——. 1997. *Proposal for a Strategic Plan for the Five-Year Period 1998–2002.* Maputo: UEM.

——. 1998. *A Project for the Third Millennium.* Maputo: UEM.

——. 1998. *Strategic Plan, 1999–2003.* Maputo: UEM.

——. 1999a. *Novo Quadro Cirricular da UEM [New Curriculum for Eduardo Mondlane University].* Maputo: UEM.

——. 1999b. *Reforma Curricular – Documento para Discussão [Curriculum Reform – Discussion Document].* Maputo: UEM.

——. 1999c. *Relatório Exames de Admissão 1999 [Report on Admission Exams 1999].* Maputo: UEM.

Edwards, E.E., M.D. Thomas, P. Rosenfeld and S. Booth-Kewley. 1997. *How to Conduct Organizational Surveys: A Step-by-Step Guide.* Thousand Oaks, CA: Sage.

Fry, P. and R. Utui. 1999. *Promoting Access, Quality and Capacity-building in African Higher Education: the Strategic Planning Experience at the Eduardo Mondlane University.* Washington, DC: ADEA Working Group on Higher Education,

Holsinger, D., P. Fry, V. Massingue, G. Moniquela and B. Cherinda. 1994. *Estudo sobre o Ensino Superior em Moçambique* [Study of Higher Education in Mozambique]. Maputo: World Bank.

Matos, Narciso. 1993. *Eduardo Mondlane University: An Experience in University Reform.* Technical Department Africa Region. Washington, DC: World Bank.

Republic of Mozambique. 1995. *Política Nacional de Educação e Estratégias de Implementação* [National Educational Policy and Implementation Strategies]. Maputo: Ministry of Education.

——. 2000. *Strategic Plan of Higher Education in Mozambique, 2000-2010.* Maputo: Ministry of Higher Education, Science and Technology.

——. n.d. *Reflexão sobre a Expansão do Ensino Superior em Moçambique* [Reflection on the Expansion ot Higher Education in Mozambique]. Maputo: Republic of Mozambique.

Silva, P. and R. Utui. 1997. *The Opinion of Some Members of the Government on Higher Education and the UEM.* Maputo: UEM.

UNESCO. 1993, 1996, 1998. *Statistical Yearbook.* Paris.

Wield, D.A., A. Bay, S. Gustafsson and P. Mlama. 1998. *Swedish Support to University Eduardo Mondlane in Mozambique.* Stockholm: Swedish International Development Agency.